21 SECRETS FOR IRRIGATION CONTRACTORS

How to Make Your Company
A Marketing Powerhouse

Copyright© 1995 by Robin Tulleners

Published in Dallas, TX by Weather-matic Publications

Printed in the United States of America

First Printing 1995

ISBN 0-9635096-1-6

TRADEMARKS

ABOUT THE AUTHOR

I want to share with you my 21 secrets for making more money. Some of the ideas will be totally new to you. Some are just plain common sense. But all of them are sound ideas — and they've been proven in real life situations. There are four reasons that qualify me to teach you how to make more money.

FIRST, I have a formal education. I attended California State Polytechnic University School of Horticulture, San Luis Obispo. My specialty was landscape contracting. Many landscape contractors who did not receive any formal training may scoff at the idea of a college degree. So did I — until I got one. My degree has been the foundation of my success. Knowledge always is.

SECOND, I have practical experience. I was President and owner of R. M. Tulleners Landscape, Inc. for 17 years. I built that business from scratch without seed money. I developed sales to over $3 million a year with a staff of four full-time salespeople, one office manager and 50 field crew members.

THIRD, I have a wide range of experiences. My business operation consisted of commercial, residential and custom home landscape installation. In fact, the Tulleners Companies was comprised of three companies: R.M. Tulleners Landscape, Inc., Centurion Iron Works, Inc. and Precision Carpentry Company.

FOURTH, I have made a lot of money as a landscape contractor. During those years as President, I averaged $150,000 (or more) in annual take home pay. This is the money that I kept, money that went into my pocket.

I have lots of valuable secrets to share with you. I've taken my money-making ideas and put them into this workbook. I hope it brings you the BIG MONEY you deserve!

Robin Tulleners, Author

AUTHOR'S PREFACE

This book was written to apply to you whether you do irrigation only or are a landscape/irrigation contractor. The methods that are explained were developed and utilized by me. I also consulted with other successful companies nationwide that confirmed that my practices are sound. *These methods successfully increased my business by over 335% in 3 short years.*

This is a step by step guide that will steer you through the marketing and sales processes. A sort of training manual, if you will. Often we go to these high dollar sales and marketing "gurus" that pump us up and get us on fire, but without a plan or road map as to how this is to be accomplished. What I offer is a plan that is easy to read, easy to follow, and at a reasonable price.

Success is not an event, it is a process.

My first idea is to build your business in a more methodical form that will be more profitable. The name of the game is not how much volume you do, but how much you keep at the end of the day. Uncontrolled growth usually is the kiss of death for most companies. It is my recommendation that you take things slowly and easily. What I offer here is equivalent to eating an elephant. We can do it; one bite at a time.

The second idea is to build the relationship between you and your clients, retaining them in a favorable fashion. Doing this will enable you to sell them again at some other time in the future, or to make use of them as an endorser for prospective customers. You must learn to coddle, nurture, and treat your clients like the gold that they truly are. You must remember that these people are the very lifeblood of your sustenance. If you do not treat them kindly, eventually word will get around and they will do business with those contractors who *do* take care of them.

The third idea is to offer some new possibilities to those of you who are truly interested in the marketing and sales process. For the sake of argument, **marketing** means the approach, or way of introducing yourself and your company's services to your prospective clients and **sales** means interacting with those prospective clients. **Closing** is the completion of the sales cycle: the exchange of money for your products or services. *Now* is the time for you to get an edge up on your competition and make that move.

My fourth thought is that you seek expert advice as required from within and outside your industry. It is impossible to know all and be all. No matter what your knowledge or experience level is, we can always learn something from the encounters of others. I also found it beneficial to be active in professional associations. They can help you with technical know-how, discounts on insurance packages, and introduce you to suppliers of the highest quality materials. It is my recommendation that you get to know and work very closely with your suppliers whose marketing plans and products support your company goals and business philosophy.

Some of your competitors will be buying this guide, too, but will do nothing with this new information. I have a friend that has been to more sales and marketing seminars than anyone. When he comes home from these things, the man is on fire! This enthusiasm soon turns to fizzle because he lacks discipline to implement the new found ideas.

I encourage you to move, but to move in a slow and methodical fashion. You did not build your business overnight. Employing these methods should be done in the same manner. At the very least, this should open your eyes and mind to the other possibilities that are available to you. As I found, contractors generally tend to be very good at what they do; they just are not good salespeople and do little else in the way of advanced thinking or expansion. I wish you good luck as you embark on this new adventure.

Robin Tulleners, Author

PUBLISHER'S FOREWORD

In 1945, Max Eldon Snoddy moved from Indiana to Dallas, Texas, to install lawn irrigation systems for affluent homeowners and businesses.

Unable to find quality sprinkler system components for his customers, Max opened his own machine shop. By the mid 1950's, he had developed and patented a myriad of new and better ideas including the first electric solenoid valve and automatic controller, and the first matched precipitation spray nozzle.

I was privileged to join the Weather-matic Division of Telsco Industries as Chief Operating Officer at the commencement of the company's 50th Anniversary celebration. During the months that followed, I spent a great deal of time "dusting off" company archives to determine the guiding principles of business philosophy which had enabled our company to prosper for half a century.

What I discovered was that innovative, quality products were only a small part of the company's success plan.

Max Snoddy believed that "a company succeeds by helping its customers be successful." Somehow, he found time between patent applications to develop contractor manuals dealing with every aspect of business philosophy (i.e., customer and vendor relations), financial management (i.e., cost accounting and ratios), sales (i.e., presentation techniques) and service (i.e., maintenance procedures). Additionally, he coauthored the first edition of THE TURF IRRIGATION MANUAL, the industry's first complete guide to landscape irrigation design . . . all completed prior to 1960.

In the 1960s, the C.I.K. (College of Irrigation Knowledge) was established to provide the finest in design training. These classes continue today.

Over 55,000 copies of THE TURF IRRIGATION MANUAL are currently in use worldwide and it was our privilege to release a new 5th Edition of the book, authored by Richard B. Choate, as part of our 50th Anniversary celebration.

As we begin our second 50 years at the threshold of the 21st Century, we see unlimited possibilities for the continued expansion of our industry. However, I am dismayed by industry statistics which indicate that 90% of the contractors in business today will fail before the year 2000! In addition, most contracting companies build few or no assets to pass on to heirs of the company founder.

I believe the reason for this appalling failure rate is that while most contractors are adequate or above average installers, they simply lack training in management and sales techniques to sustain their business. Additionally, contractors must compete with the new philosophy of many manufacturers seeking to increase their sales. Although these manufacturers will give design and installation assistance, they fail to help the contractor with the basic training needed to stay in business. Besides that, they make matters worse. By selling to the direct competitors of contractors, the mass merchandisers, manufacturers destroy markets, mutualize territories, and encourage low quality and a do-it-yourself attitude.

There is an answer. The answer is knowledge.

We have found a person who is uniquely qualified and willing to share that knowledge with you. Robin Tulleners is a successful irrigation and landscape contractor who has taken 17 years of experience and recorded it in an easy-to-understand workbook.

As an additional part of our 50th Anniversary, Weather-matic commissioned Robin to prepare this unique business guide for our industry. You, too, can be successful by understanding and applying these 21 Secrets.

I'm personally committed to help you succeed and I believe these secrets will work! Coming from a diverse background including manufacturing and finance, I have seen many of the core principles in this book used by the most successful people in business today. **If you don't find at least one idea in each chapter that will make your company more successful, I'll gladly refund the purchase price of the book.**

Sincerely,

L. Michael Mason
Vice President/Chief Operating Officer
Weather-matic

READ ME FIRST

This guide covers numerous aspects of the sales and marketing process of the irrigation industry.

First, it is my recommendation that you skim through this book to get a general feel as to the direction it is heading.

Second, you will need to go back and thoroughly read each chapter individually. It will be necessary to read slowly so as not to miss out on any of the minor details. I would encourage you to fill out the forms and develop specific plans for your business. The real success of this guide will be when you interact with it.

Third, at the end of each chapter is a Summary and ACTION PLAN. For you to realize your full potential as an irrigation contractor, it is my wish that you would develop a plan to follow up on these. I recommend that you do not proceed to the next **Step** until you feel confident that you are in full command of the current step.

GOOD LUCK!

CONTENTS

	STEPS	PAGE
Set Your Personal Goals	1	1
Establish Your Business Philosophy	2	3
Get Your License	3	11
Discover Your U.S.P.	4	15
Define Your Market	5	19
Learn to Communicate	6	31
Different Personality Types	7	35
How to Listen	8	39
The Sales Kit	9	43
Three Types of Calls	10	49
Building the Sale	11	79
Buying Signals	12	93
Set Up a Sales Staff	13	95
How to Hire a Salesperson	14	99
The Telephone as a Tool	15	107
The Fax Machine as a Tool	16	113
The Computer as a Tool	17	117
Continued Communication	18	125
Job Completion Survey	19	135
Post Lost Job Survey	20	139
Alternate Sources of Income	21	143

STEP 1

SET YOUR PERSONAL GOALS

Set specific goals

If you want to be successful at this business or anything else in life, it is imperative that you set specific personal goals. If you don't, you will be at the mercy of those who do set goals. This industry is highly competitive, but what industry isn't? Either you will eat, or be eaten, by the others that are implementing their goals.

Your personal self image is the key. Take pride in what you do, how you speak, how you appear and definitely with whom you socialize. You want to be perceived as the solution to your customer's problem. Since your company will be supporting you for many years to come, it is best to start early in learning how to make a favorable impression.

If you want to be an eagle, you must fly with them first.

Make a list of your best accomplishments, victories, and work you are proud of. This will be very uplifting. We live in a very negative and pessimistic society. We need to remind ourselves of the fruits of our past achievements. But: we cannot live on past accomplishments forever. We need to continually strive for new ideas and larger goals.

We cannot live on past accomplishments forever

Make a list of your liabilities, traits, and/or things that you desire to change. This must be done before you set your goals. Take this list of "bads" and mentally burn it. Doing this will help you clear your mind as to the direction you will go. All too often we hang onto excess baggage and drag

Eliminate the excuses and get on with the business at hand

it wherever we go. We use it as an excuse as to why we cannot achieve a particular task or goal. "If only this did not happen to me 5 years ago." It is time that you eliminate the excuses and get on with the business at hand.

Define your goals by what you want and what you want to be. You must be specific. These goals must have a purpose and will probably revolve around social, family, financial, physical, or mental issues. Make sure you not only set short and long term goals, but be realistic. Make sure some of the goals are attainable. Especially the ones that are of a short time frame. There is nothing wrong with being ambitious, but setting out to irrigate a 36-hole golf course when you haven't even done a small residence is a little ridiculous. Having too big of a goal and not being able to attain it will only end in frustration. We need short, intermediate, and long term goals. Example: 1 month, first quarter, 6 months, 1 year, 5 years. It is important that you plan your work and work your plan. Before you arrive at the job site, you should have a plan of action to properly put your men and materials to work in order to maximize your profit potential. You should run your life no differently.

We need short, intermediate, and long term goals

Summary: Having goals causes us to focus and have a sense of direction.

✔ ACTION PLAN

Write down your personal goals and affix a time frame that they are to be accomplished. Monitor these goals on a regular basis and make adjustments as necessary.

STEP 2

ESTABLISH YOUR BUSINESS PHILOSOPHY

Having the correct business philosophy can be very much like target shooting. The further you are away from your target, the harder to see the mark. Small deviations either left, right, up or down will drastically increase the chance of completely missing the bull's eye. The right philosophy, if developed and followed as a guiding beacon in the day to day conduct of your business, will contribute immeasurably to your success and allow you to be right on target.

Philosophy in business may be defined as the attitude and conduct of the owner and employees which eventually become molded into the firm's character. It is the way of business life. It is the very art of doing business. The success of your company will be in direct proportion to how well it's products and services are accepted by your clients. This acceptance will be influenced to a very large extent by the image that you create for your firm.

Moral integrity is the cornerstone foundation on which your company should be built. By definition: adherence to a set of values that enable you to differentiate between right and wrong. In other words, **when your actions equal your words.** I've found that deceit, dishonesty, and the evasion of responsibility are the surest way to quick failure. Their opposites, morality and integrity, are the primary principles of a successful business and personal philosophy. In order for your company to become successful, you must be good

Moral integrity is the cornerstone foundation on which your company should be built

3

at what you do and perform a needed service at a reasonable profit. In short, there must be ample justification for your company's existence.

If you are currently operating an irrigation business or considering starting one of your own, you must ask yourself these simple questions:

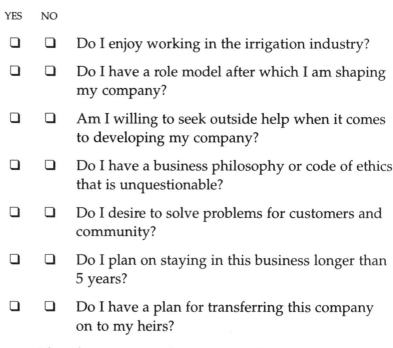

YES	NO	
❑	❑	Do I enjoy working in the irrigation industry?
❑	❑	Do I have a role model after which I am shaping my company?
❑	❑	Am I willing to seek outside help when it comes to developing my company?
❑	❑	Do I have a business philosophy or code of ethics that is unquestionable?
❑	❑	Do I desire to solve problems for customers and community?
❑	❑	Do I plan on staying in this business longer than 5 years?
❑	❑	Do I have a plan for transferring this company on to my heirs?

Identifying your goals as an irrigation contractor is an essential part of establishing your Business Plan. Planning ahead and mapping a strategy is just one aspect of a sound business philosophy. Every business follows a course, planned or otherwise. Some do it more deliberately, intelligently, and unerringly than others. I don't believe in blind fate. I have found that you have two choices in life . . . you either determine your own course or others will do it for you.

Identifying your goals as an irrigation contractor is an essential part of establishing your Business Plan

---

Robin's Law: Your company's future is determined by your decisions, not by the environment or circumstances.

The distinct advantage of pre-planning is that it minimizes waste, avoids pitfalls and adversity. Don't allow your company to be tossed about like a rudderless ship in a storm. Get the proper tools and lay the course. No wonder there are so many firms that excel at nothing and wander about aimlessly. These individuals have never taken the time to locate the tools, or invest in what it takes to rise to the top in their trade (education, associates, etc.). You would rather be like the top 5%, not the mediocre 95%. It's worth the effort.

POINT NUMBER ONE: ATTITUDE TOWARD CUSTOMERS

Your attitude toward your customers can be a precious asset or a disastrous liability for your company and it's ultimate success. This will be the single most important point of your philosophy. The following **Twelve Commandments of Good Business**, paraphrased by me and advocated by the Better Business Bureau should be made as unbreakable rules for you and your employees.

- Your Customer is the most important person in your business.

- Your Customer is not dependent on you—you are dependent on your Customer.

- Your Customer is not an interruption of your work—the Customer is the purpose of it.

- Your Customer does *you* a favor when he or she calls.

- Your Customer is a part of your business—not an outsider.

- Your Customer is not a cold statistic—he or she is a flesh and blood human being with emotions like your own.

- Your Customer is not someone with whom to argue or match wits.

- Your Customer is a person who brings you their wants—it is your job to fill those wants.

- Your Customer is deserving of the most courteous and attentive treatment you can give.

- Your Customer makes it possible to pay your salary.

- Your Customer is the lifeblood of your business.

- Your Customer likes to trade with a company that supports the community.

POINT NUMBER TWO: ATTITUDE TOWARD EMPLOYEES

The second most important facet of your philosophy will be your attitude toward your employees. Unless you work alone, it is very crucial to screen and hire the employees that best fit your attitude and philosophy.

You must earn their respect and understanding by treating them the same way you would like to be treated. They should be held accountable for fulfilling **"well defined job functions and work standards."** They must be required to comply with company policies and abide by the rules.

It is very crucial to screen and hire the employees that best fit your attitude and philosophy

If the boss sets the pace with hard work, strong business ethics, accountability and moral integrity, the employees will follow suit

Treat your employees fairly but firmly. A fair day's pay for a fair day's work should be the rule rather than the exception. An atmosphere of mutual respect, understanding and cooperation should prevail throughout your organization. I call this "top down" management. If the boss sets the pace with hard work, strong business ethics, accountability and moral integrity, the employees will follow suit.

You must find employees with "heart." This characteristic is most often reflected by a spring in the step, a smile on the face and an attitude to service. It is important to hire employees who love their work and their position — craftsmen at their trade. They should have a passion for installing irrigation and problem solving. Utilizing temporary workers may help you out of your short term jam but could lead to long term aggravation. If you have a good feeling while you're around your employees, that's probably a sign that your customers will feel the same way. The importance of this is that your customers should enjoy doing business with your company and dealing with your employees. The reward will be lifetime customers.

Encourage self improvement through trade sources and outside educational means

Most employees are ambitious when given the opportunity to improve themselves and upgrade their own abilities. Encourage self improvement through trade sources and outside educational means. Continually train, retrain, and upgrade your people. Encourage employees in their belief that they are an essential part of your business and have a personal stake in it. We all have a feeling of wanting to "belong."

Robin's Tip: Help your employees to understand that their job has a greater meaning than just designing and installing irrigation. As environmental team members, they are creating beauty, saving water and helping to clean the air.

7

POINT NUMBER THREE: ATTITUDE TOWARD SUPPLIERS

The third most important facet of your philosophy is the attitude of your company toward its suppliers. The supplier's ability to influence your success should not be underestimated or taken for granted. It is my recommendation that you establish a sound and lasting relationship with your major suppliers, especially those that you depend on most for the bulk of your material supplies. Treat them with respect, pay your bills on time and communicate your needs to them. By doing these small items, you will build loyalty, receive additional service and benefits and have the supplier as a valuable team member.

Here are my three rules for strategic use of suppliers:

1. Minimize the number of suppliers you use.

   This allows you to concentrate your buying power. The Pros call this "taking advantage of economies of scale." You want to be a "big fish in a small dependable pond." Your business must be important to them.

2. Select and support suppliers who are committed to help you build your business and support your industry.

   Choose companies that are dedicated to the needs of the professional contractor. Ask your suppliers and manufacturers how they intend to grow and at whose expense. Ask yourself, do these growth plans help or hurt your business and your industry. For example, how are you affected by irrigation related manufacturers who are relying on home centers and other do-it-yourself outlets to fuel their strategic growth plans?

3. Choose suppliers who help secure sales for your company and provide management and technical assistance.

Summary: Establishing positive business values, ethics and relationships between you, your employees and your suppliers early in your career is extremely beneficial.

✔ ACTION PLAN

Institute your business philosophy. Develop your guidelines between you, your customers and your employees. Research and locate your primary suppliers that meet the targets outlined in Point Number Three.

NOTES

STEP 3

GET YOUR LICENSE

This sales and marketing training manual is written for both seasoned contractors and first timers. The main idea of this book is not only to educate but to promote professionalism. Everyone knows that contractors have a bad and tarnished image. If you don't believe me, just for fun go rent a couple of videos. "The Money Pit" and "Tin Men" will give you a sense of what I'm talking about.

For those of you who are already licensed, feel free to move on to the next step. For those who aren't, listen carefully. GET YOUR LICENSE! Contact your local state license board and find out when the next test date is, have them send out the application form and then start studying.

Recommended reading is your State License Law Book. Have fun. In California 50% of the test is based on license law and the other 50% on actual contracting specifics like irrigation design, sprinkler quantities, plant types, and the like. Certain states like Texas and Florida require irrigators to be licensed. I also recommend that you consider getting certified by the Irrigation Association (IA) or joining the local trade association. Doing so will definitely improve your image as a professional. You must however, check your state license board for other local requirements.

One of my employers during college, helped me get qualified for my license. These are the guys you need to vouch for you and your actual on-the-job experience. He was never licensed, but owned a ranch and did a lot of contractor work-related things. He was wondering if he would be able to pass the contractor's exam. After taking the exam, I said "definitely not." The reason being: that without some sort of formal training or tutoring school, the test is far too complex to fake it. You only would end up frustrated.

If you have a formal education from a college or university that specializes in contracting, you should not have any trouble. If you have been working for a contractor and now you wish to be on your own, hire one of the tutoring contractor licensing schools, pay the fees, study like crazy and go take the test.

As a contractor, the license is not only a legal requirement but an integral part of your sales and marketing program. Believe it or not, there are many individuals out there who are operating without a license and taking money out of your pocket by doing so. You need to be licensed as your first step. This puts you one notch above the rest.

Once you become licensed, you will need to come up with a name and business cards. Depending on the image that you want to convey, all sorts of card styles and type are available. My recommendation is to find yourself a discount printer that will give you a little flexibility as far as the design and layout of your pertinent information. Try to stay away from the universally-applicable, mass-marketed "man with a wheelbarrow" business card. Have your printer put 5 of your best selling points on the back of the card. This can be an effective tool. Try to institute a little creativity. If you are going to spring for envelopes and letterhead, make sure that they all are the same colors and type set. It will give people an impression that your firm is professional and well established. In the very least, when you mail a letter you will get a lot of pride out of seeing your name professionally done. Besides, you will save time by not having to put the return address on them.

The license is an integral part of your sales and marketing program

Try to stay away from the "man with a wheelbarrow" business card

Some states
require that any
form of
advertising
include the state
license number

Try to include all of the basics such as company name, your first and last name, address, telephone and fax number if available. **DO NOT FORGET YOUR CONTRACTOR LICENSE NUMBER!** California and several other states require that any form of advertising include the state license number. Whether your state does or does not require one, be proud and put it on there anyway. This will prevent people from asking, "Are you licensed?" Some contractors that are running their business from their residence prefer privacy and do not put their home address on the business card. If you are one of these individuals that is using a P.O. box in lieu of your home address, I found that this is a real turn off to most clients. Personally, I feel a contractor gives the wrong impression by doing so. Consumers like to deal with well established contractors. Depending on your personal situation and where you live, post office boxes can now be had at a place of business like Mail Boxes Etc. that provide a physical address. A person would never know unless they drove by to have a look.

Summary: Obtaining your license and/or certification is the only way to becoming a professional. Utilize your business card to promote yourself as a reputable, licensed and certified contractor.

✔ ACTION PLAN

Take your contractor license test, design and have your business card printed.

For more information about the national Irrigation Association Certification Program, call or write:

The Irrigation Association
8260 Willow Oaks Corporate Drive, Suite 120
Fairfax, Virginia 22031
Tel: (703) 573-3551
Fax: (703) 573-1913

NOTES

STEP 4

DISCOVER YOUR USP

This is the single most important item that you want to develop over time that will distinguish your company from the others

USP. Whaaaat? Unique Selling Proposition. This is the least thought about item that probably has the largest impact not only on your clients, but on your company as a whole. This is the single most important item that you want to develop over time that will distinguish your company from the others. Typically, contractors get lumped into a massive pool and are known as a commodity. Different company name, same services, same crew, same price, same, same, same. It is imperative that you develop characteristics that will change you and your company into a proprietary operation. USP is what you tell customers when they say, "Why should I use ABC Irrigation?"

A few examples of highly successful USP's are: "When you absolutely, positively have to have it by 10:30am." Federal Express coined this slogan. "Hot pizza delivered to your home in 30 minutes or it's free." You guessed it, Domino's Pizza.

These companies built entire empires as well as fortunes around their USP. These are the things that enabled them to carve out a market niche and make their firms different from all of the other freight and pizza delivery companies.

Some USP's can be based on what you are currently doing in the market place— such as custom residential specialist, or quick response time or whatever. If you have a Unique Selling Proposition but are not verbalizing it, you should. One of the places to do it is on your business card. Beware though, a USP or slogan can backfire on you if you do not deliver what you profess.

15

Look carefully at ways to distinguish your firm from the others

As you take a look at what your company's strengths are, look carefully at some powerful ways to truly distinguish your firm from the others. Some people try to think up this slogan over night. I recommend developing this USP over a period of time so that your focus will be well thought out and not haphazardly applied. I know you will be excited about this, just take your time and work on a message that best fits you particular circumstance. This slogan will be with you for a very long time, it is not something that gets changed once a year.

Make sure that you get your entire staff involved. Have them participate as to what some of the company's strengths are and how they can be built into a major marketing theme. A good way to get started is to look in the Yellow Pages and make a checklist of the different USP's from the different companies. By doing this investigative work, you will be able to see if your competition has good USP's or if they are generic like, "We do quality work." This, too, will show you what not to use.

Unique Selling Proposition Examples

1. _____

2. _____

3. _____

4. _____

5. _____

YOUR Unique Selling Proposition

_____

If you do some sort of advertising in a magazine, Yellow Pages, or newspaper, make sure that you expand on

Stress why you
are better than
others

your slogan in the body of the ad. Announcing that at ABC Irrigation, "We do irrigation right," is far better than merely using your name. I recommend that you explain *why* you do irrigation right. Something like, "Our technicians are all certified by the Irrigation Association which means that your job will be installed at the highest standards set by the industry," or, "Using an insured contractor sure has its benefits. No claims, no sleepless nights, no grief. Period!" OR, "To maximize customer satisfaction, each job is person-ally certified and signed off by the company owner *and* designer on our 20 point quality control inspection that is endorsed by the Irrigation Association."

See the difference? You want to stress *why* you are better than others. Remember: the prospective clients can not read your mind. It is a little extra work, but the profits will return the effort many times over.

Summary: Unique Selling Propositions help distinguish your company from the others.

✔ ACTION PLAN

Involve your company personnel in helping you develop a main marketing theme or slogan. Make sure you advocate this slogan at all levels in your company. Be sure to print it on your business card.

NOTES

STEP 5

DEFINE YOUR MARKET

Going under the assumption that you are currently in operation and things are running along okay, you now have made up your mind that you want to do a little expansion. The reasons could vary. For me they were ambition, time to step up to the next level of business, spending too much time at work and time to delegate some of these responsibilities to others. And of course, as an entrepreneur, the goal of increased income is always a tremendous motivation!

When talking to contractors, they invariably say "I just want to grow bigger." Or "I want to make more money." Most of them don't have an idea what it takes to do either one. They just know that is what they want. Period.

The problem is, blind ambition without a sense of direction can be fatal. For example, one fellow told me he was earning $1.5 million dollars a year in gross sales and was taking home $30,000 a year for himself personally. He felt that he had the world by the tail and was calling the shots. I said to myself, "Where else in the world can you be self employed, work 70-80 hours per week, have all of that liability, and make 50% less than you could if you were working for someone else?" Well, this was my recommendation to him: quit the business and go to work for someone else. Apparently he was able to get the business, but none of it was profitable.

The following is a questionnaire to help you think a little about some things that need to be considered prior to going wild with your sales and marketing program.

INFORMATION REQUIRED TO DEFINE A MARKETING STRATEGY FOR IRRIGATION CONTRACTORS

Applies to both installation and maintenance contractors.

Briefly describe your goals.

1. _____

2. _____

3. _____

Have you ever drafted a mission statement that epitomizes these goals? If yes, please state its contents. _____

_____

What is your business philosophy and how does it relate to your customers?

_____

_____

_____

_____

_____

_____

_____

Do you have a Unique Selling Proposition or slogan that separates your company from others?

If so, what is it? _____

What is your current client mix?

_____ % Institutions

_____ % Small Businesses

_____ % Large Businesses

_____ % Residential (homeowners)

_____ % City, County, State, Federal Government

_____ % Reconstruction

_____ % Others _____

Which type do you prefer? _____

Why? _____

Which areas would you like to expand into and capitalize on? _____

_____

Why do you feel that this is the area for expansion? _____

Number in order of importance the items you consider appropriate for a marketing budget.

_____ Ads in metropolitan newspapers

_____ Ads in local, small city newspapers

_____ Ads in Penny Saver type publications

_____ Ads in retirement community newspapers

_____ Ads in community arts/schools/sports programs

_____ Pamphlets, fliers

_____ Brochures, business cards

_____ TV, radio

_____ Home and Garden shows

_____ Direct mail, direct mail address lists

_____ Door hangars

_____ Telemarketing

_____ Fax Communications

_____ Sales personnel, representatives

_____ Yellow Pages

_____ Special events, seminars, etc. for specifiers and related professionals

_____ Christmas gifts

_____ Give away promotional items

_____ Other _____

Which of the above areas are you currently utilizing and how are they working?

_____

_____

_____

_____

_____

_____

What percentage of your budget is allocated to each? _____

_____

_____

_____

_____

_____

_____

Where should you begin to look for persons wanting a contractor? Indicate where you think you should start by numbering the examples below in order of their importance .

_____ Property managers

_____ Material supplier bulletin board

_____ Institutions (banks, colleges, restaurants)

_____ Loan executives

_____ Realtors

_____ Landscape architects

_____ Building architects

_____ Purchasing agents for city, state, federal government

_____ Retirement communities

_____ Rotary, Lions, Chamber of Commerce, etc.

_____ Green Sheet, Construction Marketing Data, other published papers listing new projects for bid, etc.

_____ General contractors

_____ Builders, developers

_____ Related trade associations

_____ Unrelated trade associations

_____ Neighbors

_____ Homeowner associations

_____ Other _____

How do you propose to contact these potential clients? _____

_____

What is your method of showing your potential clients your completed jobs?

_____

List the items that this format contains. (e.g., photos, slide show, video, etc.)_____

_____

Do you have prepared lists or testimonials from satisfied clients, classified by type, to give to a potential customer of the same type so that they can reference your credibility?   _____

Name the routine technical services you offer a client, (sprinklers, soil preparation, trees, hardscape, etc.) and indicate whether you normally hire skilled tradesmen and supervise them yourself or subcontract these skills out.

ROUTINE TECHNICAL SERVICES PERFORMED	HIRE	SUBCONTRACT
1. _____		
2. _____		
3. _____		
4. _____		
5. _____		

Do you steer your customers to a particular loan executive if they need financial help?_____

If you steer clients to a particular loan officer or institution, do you receive a commission for this? _____

Do you provide non-technical services, (preparation for a client loan, permit processing?) _____

Are there any non-technical services that you could provide if the service were properly developed and presented?_____ If either answer is yes, please describe below the services that you offer or would offer.

_____

_____

_____

_____

Describe the typical payment schedule that you propose to the client.

_____ % Down

_____ % When materials are on site

_____ % Upon completion

_____ % After guarantee period

_____ % Retention

_____ % Other _____

Do you routinely check a client's credit? _____

How? _____

Do you use a pre-printed standardized bid form? _____

Do you use a pre-printed standardized contract? _____

Briefly outline the steps in a typical job from the moment the client is contacted to the last payment.

1. _____

2. _____

3. _____

4. _____

5. _____

6. _____

7. _____

8. _____

9. _____

10. _____

How many months do you normally guarantee your work? _____

What type of estimating software do you use or do you do it by hand? _____

_____

Is there a business relationship between you and the architects you use in the way of commissions? _____

Have you ever offered an architect a commission for business sent your way? _____

_____

Has any government official asked you for a kick back or finders fee? _____

If not, would you consider the thought? _____

Do you share marketing expenses with any of your suppliers? _____

Do you know any contractors who utilize a unique marketing concept? _____

If so, what is it? _____

Do you have any financial limits?_____ If yes, what are they?

1. _____

2. _____

How many permanent employees?_____ Part time employees? _____

How many are considered as office or managerial? _____

What types of insurance coverage and what limits do you carry?

TYPE   COVERAGE

1. _____

2. _____

3. _____

4. _____

5. _____

If your business expanded by 100% tomorrow, from a practical viewpoint, could you adequately provide the foremen, skilled part time employees, equipment, funds, etc. to satisfy the old and new customers alike?

_____

Prioritize by describing in order of importance, responsibilities that a salesperson should tackle first.

1. _____

2. _____

3. _____

4. _____

5. _____

If a person were to fulfill the responsibilities outlined above, select from the list below a plan for compensating that person.

1. A monthly salary

2. A monthly salary with_____ % company bonus based on net profit

3. A monthly salary with_____ % commission on gross sales and an expense account, no bonus

4. A $_____/month draw against_____ % of the gross sales and an expense account

5. _____ % of the gross contract price and an expense account

If the salesperson develops a lead that turns into a contract, is he/she guaranteed the same rate of compensation from all future contracts from that client? _____

_____

Once the salesperson is hired, for tax purposes, how would he/she be identified?

_____ Employee

_____ Self employed independent contractor

_____ Other _____

If the compensation includes expenses, which items are supplied by company and which are reimbursable to salesperson?

	COMPANY	SALESPERSON
Office equipment repairs	_____	_____
Auto use $___/mile	_____	_____
Gas, oil, repairs	_____	_____
Postage, UPS, etc.	_____	_____
Misc. office supplies	_____	_____
Meals	_____	_____
Business cards, forms	_____	_____
Telephone calls from home or car	_____	_____
Health Insurance	_____	_____
Vacation Pay	_____	_____

What is monthly maximum on reimbursable expenses? _____

At what dollar value is permission needed for a particular expense? _____

✔ ACTION PLAN

Summary: Understanding that there is more to sales and lead generation than comes to mind.

Fill out questionnaire and contemplate the direction and at what pace the growth should take place. Develop a time line for accomplishing certain tasks.

NOTES

STEP 6

LEARN TO COMMUNICATE

Be face to face
with the client

It is very easy to have the client misinterpret what you say due to lack of communication. Communication is the exchange of ideas, information and feelings with understanding and acceptance. I found it far more effective and valuable to be face to face with the client. When dealing with people over the phone, you will be unable to read facial expressions, body language, and the like. Even though someone may agree in principle with what you say by exerting an " uh, huh," it is his look of bewilderment that will enable you to see that he is truly confused on the last point that you were trying to make. Besides, the more you are in front of them, the better the opportunity to build rapport, trust, credibility and lower the apprehension that they have of you.

> *Robin's Law: As a rule, the higher the price of what you are selling, or the more sophisticated the buyer, the more detailed explanation will be needed.*

If the client says, "The price is too high," he is telling you that is not what he wants for the price you have quoted. Did they understand what you were giving them? However, it has been my experience that when *selling*, (notice, not bidding), if your price is higher, a full detailed explanation of the difference in value that you are offering the client *must* be given. Too often the client assumes that everyone submitting a proposal will include valve boxes, backflow devices and swing joints. **As a contractor, it is your responsibility to fully explain each item that will go into the job.** There is a

Explain things thoroughly and slowly

difference in design, products and warranty with each irrigation system. Most of the time, the client has no clue what the architect has outlined in the plans and specifications. People communicate when they alternately send and receive messages which are mutually beneficial.

When communicating with anyone, explain things thoroughly and slowly since your customers are hearing this for the first time. Hopefully your commercial clients have been down this path before and the terminology is not foreign to them.

A way to demonstrate this is with your workers.

1. Tell them what you want done and how it is to be done.

2. Show them how it is to be done.

3. Ask them to tell you what and how you want it done.

4. Have them show you how to do it.

5. If they do it incorrectly, repeat until successfully completed.

People think in terms of pictures, words only trigger pictures. At your next sales presentation, let the customer program the sprinkler controller that will be used on their job. This demo unit can be operated by using an alkaline battery or simply plugging it into the wall socket. You will be amazed at how your client will respond by being allowed to participate with its operation.

FACT

The human brain can think 4 times faster than anyone can talk. Try to talk behind the client. Think ahead so that you are in control. New knowledge enters the brain by sight 83% of the time. Listening is "seeing" what one hears.

FACT

Average attention span is between 0 and 8 seconds. A way to increase and hold the clients attention is by using their name. Example: Jim, Debbie, Dr. Jones.

People are interested in themselves. Every human being needs to be right and longs to be understood. Most irrigation sales are lost because the contractor offers a solution before they fully understand the problem. For example, if the client says, "What would you do with overspray on the concrete?" The rule here is to ask more questions before you answer. Keep calm, don't overreact to the situation. Most of the time he/she is merely on a fact finding mission. Remember, this is probably his/her first job and he/she is unfamiliar with the spray patterns. Don't always assume that you have to adjust the entire system! Demonstrate willingness to listen, use eye contact. Some recommended dialogue might include, "Do you mind if I ask you another question, Allen?" Using the customer's name keeps his attention and helps him feel that he is important. The person who asks the questions controls the conversation.

Summary: Proper communication is the cornerstone of successful sales.

Sales are lost because the contractor offers a solution before they fully understand the problem

✔ ACTION PLAN

Learn how to speak slowly, confidently, and in detail to clients.

NOTES

STEP 7

DIFFERENT PERSONALITY TYPES

Learn what type of personality you are working with

In order *to become* a successful salesperson or to direct your sales staff to closing deals, I cannot stress enough the importance of learning what type of personality you are working with. People are not clones and it is your goal to identify in what way they differ. Some of this can be done by looking at their surroundings, how they live, and what they drive. Other ways are through carefully selecting the right kind of questions that will help you build a small personality profile of your client. Armed with this information, you will learn the buying habits and selection processes of the people you deal with.

You must remember, we are *not* doing manipulative selling. There is no substitute for your likable personality. People will start to pick up on the fact if indeed you are trying to manipulate them into a sale. Besides, those are the antics of non-professionals.

AMIABLE

These folks are good listeners, like to be dealt with on a first name basis, are very easily manipulated, do not like to take risks, like to feel as if they are part of the group. Never rush these people, you must communicate patience to them. **Occupations:** social worker, secretary

ANALYTICAL

This particular group wants to know how it works, they strive for perfection, and are quality-oriented and are non-risk takers. Never say or use the word "quality." Do not give them two choices, you may be in for a long haul if you do. Make sure you supply them with plenty of literature. Be prepared to answer plenty of questions. Don't rush to make a decision. They are not too casual. Maintain professional, business like manner. List advantages and disadvantages. **Occupations:** engineers, scientists

DRIVERS

These people for the most part are risk takers, need to achieve, don't go slowly. Time is extremely important, they are quantity oriented, and work oriented. It's OK to initiate action but don't make the decision for them. Give them options, they usually have large egos. **Occupations:** Doctors, lawyers, executives, corporate heads

EXPRESSIVE

These people need to be recognized, try to laugh at their jokes. They are high energy individuals, are sloppy, make good sales people, are fun-loving and tend to exaggerate. **Occupations:** Entertainment, arts, sales

NON-VERBAL COMMUNICATION

It is very important to keep in the back of your mind subtle body movements that your prospective client makes that could help you land the contract. These movements are called "body language." Crossed arms are defensive, elbows on the table are confidence, crossed legs, kicking or doodling is boredom, the sideways glance is a sign of suspicion. Customers who look you in the eyes are confident people and self doubting people use their hands to talk. When a nervous habit stops while the person is conversing, the client has made a decision. Jingling money is a hint of a cost conscience person or a tight wad. If the person pulls away or withdraws, he has a lack of confidence in you and you must gently lean forward to reestablish his level of confidence.

No one person is just one single personality type; he or she usually is a mixture of several. Be careful not to categorize them too quickly. The following is a list of some common personalities and how to cope with them.

TOUGH GUY/GAL

Find something that he/she is proud of and flatter them. When they act tough, it is just a defense mechanism to scare salespeople off. Ignore it.

TIMID

Explain in great detail and speak slowly, seek advice, pay a compliment.

WISE GUY/GAL

Think they are smarter. Compliment them, ask advice. Flatter them into buying.

YOUNG

Since he/she is young, you need to show respect for their opinions.

MIDDLE AGE

Compliment them on their position, accomplishments, material goods.

SENIOR CITIZEN

Show respect for their age, experience and wisdom.

TALKATIVE

Channel the conversation, they will often talk themselves into a sale if you let them.

INDIFFERENT

Need to draw them out with questions.

SARCASTIC

Remain calm. Be sincere. Disarm them with silence.

Summary: Different personality types require different methods of handling in order to for them to trust you and lower their apprehension.

✔ ACTION PLAN

Study these different types. Develop a sales strategy of how to address each type as you make your sales calls.

STEP 8

HOW TO LISTEN

The idea here is: to listen, listen, listen. God gave us two ears and one mouth for a very good reason. If you are doing all of the talking, and acting like a know it all like I used to, then you will win over very few customers. This is a very important step to your becoming a successful contractor. Granted some people like to be led by the hand through each step, but I encourage you to let them talk.

I had one client that *wanted* me to make all of the decisions. The problem *was* that my tastes and his *were* two worlds apart. You will get more respect and a more appreciative client if you allow him/her to express themselves. Clients will tell you they don't know what they want, but by using the right kind of probing questions and good listening, I have found that they really do know what they want.

PREPARE IN ADVANCE

Remarks and questions prepared in advance free your mind for listening. You need to review prior to the meeting the direction your questions will take you and what your desired response should be.

LEARN TO THINK LIKE THE CUSTOMER

His or her problems and needs are important, you will understand and retain them better if you keep their point of view. All too often we lose sight of this and try to push our agenda.

PUT LIMITS ON YOUR OWN TALKING

You can't talk and listen at the same time. Remember: listen, listen, listen.

ASK THE CUSTOMER A LOT OF QUESTIONS

You need to ask open ended questions like who, what, where, why, and how. These will force the customer to divulge more information and not allow him or her to answer "no" or "yes" only. If you don't understand something or feel you may have missed the point, clear it up now. It may embarrass you later.

TAKE COMPREHENSIVE NOTES WHILE THE CUSTOMER IS TALKING

This will help you remember important points. Be selective. Trying to note every little detail will leave you far behind and frustrated. Let the customer know that you will be taking notes.

CONCENTRATE ON THE CUSTOMER

Focus your mind on what he or she is saying. Practice shutting out outside distractions. Remember the last time you tried dealing with a salesperson that was distracted? Annoying, wasn't it?

DON'T INTERRUPT WHILE THE CUSTOMER IS TALKING

A pause, even a long pause doesn't always mean that the client has finished saying everything he or she wants. As long as they are talking, you are gaining valuable information.

"HEAR" WHAT THEY HAVE TO SAY

You want to get the whole picture, not just isolated bits and pieces.

LISTEN FOR OVERTONES

You can learn a great deal about the customer from the way he or she says things and the way they react to the things that you say.

INTERJECTIONS

An occasional, "Yes," or "I see," shows the customer you are still with them. Be careful you do not over do it. The client will pick up on your inattention.

TURN OFF YOUR OWN WORRIES

This is not always easy. Personal fears, worries, problems not connected with the customer form a kind of static that can blank out the client's message.

REACT TO IDEAS, NOT THE PERSON

Don't become irritated at the things he or she may say or do. Don't argue mentally or verbally, this battle is not worth winning. Trying to prove yourself right will never land the contract.

DON'T JUMP TO CONCLUSIONS

Avoid making unwarranted assumptions about what the customer is going to say, or mentally try to complete his or her sentences for them.

PRACTICE LISTENING

Make your conversations (with your friends, family, or the people who serve you in the places you buy), a tool for improving your listening skills.

Summary: Listening is more important than speaking.

✔ ACTION PLAN

Learn to listen, be slow to speak, practice with your family, friends, and business associates.

STEP 9

THE SALES KIT

Once you have figured out the course your company should be going, it is time to give you or your sales people the proper tools to help them navigate this course. The "sales kit" as I call it, is the tool. A warning though, unless you already have all the items needed, this will take some time to build. The kit could be an organized binder or video containing items that you wish to reinforce to your prospective client as to why they should do business with you.

The sales kit tells a story

The sales kit tells a story about who you are and some of your accomplishments. At this juncture you need to play up on your company strengths and build desire in your client to a point where they will find you irresistible. People you will be talking to will probably not have heard of you. In the event that they have, you do not know what they have heard from others. I recommend that you give the client the who you are, how you came to be, where you are located and what your company business focus and/or philosophy is. This will clear up any misconceptions that they have about your firm.

Some of the items you should incorporate are:

1. A copy of your contractors license and/or Irrigation Association certificate.

2. Certificate of liability and workers compensation insurance.

3. Contractor comparison spreadsheet. (see sample)

4. Location of your business.

5. Company vision statement or focus.

6. Client testimonials.

7. Bank and supplier references.

8. Credit report (TRW or Dunn & Bradstreet). These demonstrate your credit worthiness and financial stability.

9. Photographs of your best completed jobs.

10. Detailed pictures of one of your crews on the job installing sprinkler related items that could be of concern or interest to the client.

11. Clean up or final punchlist form

Take pictures of your work

What picture comes to mind when you think of a "city crew" working, and, why is this? What image will you convey to your customers about your crew and your operation? The photographs that you take should be representative of the type of work that you perform. Take pictures of *your* work. You never know who knows whom. Either you can do the photography yourself or you can hire it out to a professional. My personal experience was that the professional photographer charged too much and was trying to make the sites too much like Hollywood. If you are going to take the pictures, purchase a wide angle lens, get the owner's permission and make sure that the job shows well. Take photos of pertinent items. For example, show how the pop-ups work in relation to the type of lawn they are being used on; or, show the distance the sprinkler is away from the concrete so the lawn maintenance crew won't destroy them with their edging equipment; or, a professional looking controller installation; or, how well the system is adjusted to minimize overspray, etc. These pictures will help your client visualize the caliber of work you do and will make a world of difference.

It is my recommendation that when you make a proposal presentation and are trying to get a signed contract, you have the above outlined items (except for the photos) and a cover letter enclosed in a brochure that will be left with the customer. This acts as a reminder and reinforces as to why they hired you.

The chart on the following page is similar to the one Lee Iacocca used in magazine ads comparing Chrysler's car features to those of other manufacturers. This sheet can be a tremendous marketing tool. In a nutshell, it can explain some of your company's strengths that you might not necessarily be able to reel off while talking to the client. This will allow them to sit at their own leisure and compare the other contractors. These are some examples. I am sure that you can add several positive items about your company.

Another item I found to be effective is making a list of system design and installation standards and putting it into a checklist format. This will help your client match the manufacturer (quality), type and size of the components that you will use on their job and compare these parts to what the competition will be supplying (or won't).

One last component that works well is physically showing your prospective client your jobs by driving through the neighborhoods, business parks or shopping centers. This will allow them to personally inspect your work and eliminate any doubt in their mind as to whom they should do business with. I used to insist on doing this because rarely will they do it on their own. The tour will permit you to learn more about them and will allow them to feel more comfortable with you. Again, this is a little more work but well worth the effort.

Summary: The sales kit is the tool that tells about your company.

✔ ACTION PLAN

Wait for a clear day and take pictures of your best work. Start to assemble the balance of items laid out above.

CONTRACTOR COMPARISON SPREADSHEET (SAMPLE)

COMPARISON ELEMENTS	ABC IRRIGATION	OTHERS
OVER 25 YEARS IN BUSINESS	YES	
CURRENT CONTRACTORS LICENSE	YES	
LIEN RELEASE WITH PROGRESS PAYMENTS	YES	
$1 MILLION DOLLAR LIABILITY INSURANCE	YES	
WORKER'S COMPENSATION INSURANCE	YES	
STATE AWARD WINNERS	YES	
PROVEN PERFORMANCE ON SIMILAR SIZE PROJECTS	YES	
EXPERIENCED & KNOWLEDGEABLE CRAFTSMEN	YES	
TOP QUALITY MATERIALS & SUPPLIERS	YES	
SINGLE SOURCE RESPONSIBILITY	YES	
RESPONSIVE COMMUNICATIONS	YES	
COMPETITIVE PRICING	YES	
TIMELY COMPLETION	YES	
COORDINATED EFFORT OF TOTAL PICTURE	YES	
EXCELLENT SAFETY RECORD	YES	
FULL TIME OFFICE STAFF	YES	
REGULAR BUSINESS HOURS	YES	
IN HOUSE DESIGNER	YES	
COMPUTER DESIGNS (CAD)	YES	
VALUE ENGINEERING SERVICE	YES	
ENVIRONMENTALLY CONSCIENTIOUS	YES	
WRITTEN WARRANTIES	YES	
RADIO DISPATCHED TRUCKS	YES	
ANNUAL SERVICE PLANS	YES	
PAGERS FOR KEY PERSONNEL	YES	

ABC IRRIGATION CHECKLIST (SAMPLE)

ITEM	QTY	MFGR.	SIZE
Backflow	1	XYZ Company	1-1/2"
Backflow Fittings		All Brass	1-1/2"
Mainline	800 l.f.	Poly Plastics	2" class 315
Valves		W*M	
Valve Boxes			
Hose Bibs			
Quick Couplers			
Controller		W*M	
Wire/Wire Connections			
Lawn Pop-ups		W*M	
Shrub Pop-ups		W*M	
Shrub Risers		W*M	
Rotary Heads		W*M	
Riser Assembly			
Drip System			

NOTES

STEP 10

THREE TYPES OF CALLS

Now I know what you are thinking. "Yuck! I hate making cold calls. Let someone else make those calls!" Well, the fact is, you have been making them for longer than you think.

Unless you have people pounding your door down or you are not interested in any sort of expansion, then you had better pay *close* attention to this section.

Cold calls happen every day but you probably do not realize it. For example when you walk up to the next-door neighbor of a job you are working on, or stop and hand a business card to the job-site superintendent building the local shopping center, these both are forms of a cold call. These are the opportunities that you need to capitalize on. More than **95%** of the contractors out there feel like they have accomplished something if they walk up, ask the superintendent if they have hired an irrigator, hand them a business card, and retreat to the safety of their truck. First, if you are getting up the courage to talk and interrupt him or her, you had better make it a good pitch. Second, you never know if he or she is the owner, purchasing agent or whom-ever. A good first impression could favorably impress them and help sway the decision in your favor.

Reflecting back to the time I was a newspaper boy at the ripe old age of 11, the District Manager told us that if we wanted to sell newspaper subscriptions, we had to distinguish our newspaper from all of the others and we had to do

Cold calls happen every day

Opportunities to capitalize on

it with a cold call. And in the competitive Southern California market, there were many other papers vying for these ever so important subscription dollars.

I worked for a relatively small newspaper that was delivered in a modest geographic area. It was not a throwaway that you get once a week, it had more content than that and was delivered 6 days a week.

I would start by speaking slowly, giving them my full name and my employer's name. Then I told them all the different sections that this newspaper included. National news, international news, sports that covered all the major teams and especially the local high schools. It also included "Dear Abby," Letters to the Editor, and, of course, the Thursday fliers with the coupons from the local grocery stores. All of this for a paltry $1.75 per month. And that included being put on your porch! How could they resist!

My motivation was that I needed the money for the Helms Bakery truck to purchase my favorite jelly filled donut or to go on go-kart outings sponsored by the newspaper.

If you listen to the pitches today — if you actually can have someone at your front door since most now are done by telemarketing —these little kids never talk about anything except a trip to Hawaii that they are working for. Why would I want to help some kid go to Hawaii when I've never been? I want to know more about what I am about to purchase for my hard earned money. My point is that embellishing on your service will not only educate the client, but entice them to make the purchase from you since they feel that they are receiving more value for their money.

Robin's Law: Practice your cold call pitch to the point that it becomes second nature to you. The smoother your delivery, the more believable.

If your company has several crews, secretaries, etc. working for it, then those people must exude the same philosophy as you and your sales people do. This must start with the frontline secretary or crew foreman and work all the way down to the installers and service technicians.

PURPOSE

The purpose of this next sales section is to teach you some basic sales techniques.

PHILOSOPHY

The philosophy of ABC Irrigation is to do business in an honest and positive manner. All of your dealings with prospects and customers should reflect this philosophy.

Please adhere to the following guidelines.

- Never lie.

- Never disparage

    — your boss.
    — your competitors.
    — ABC Irrigation employees.

- Never get angry with a prospect or customer.

- Never quit selling.

This section presents techniques. Because sales techniques vary based on the type of sales call being made, this section divides sales calls into the three general types below:

- *The cold call.*

- *The first appointment call.*

- *The closing call.*

Several special situations that may occur are also discussed. Since a salesperson always is confronted with objections during a call, this section also presents common objections and suggests answers.

Finally, this section discusses several general sales techniques that apply to any selling situation.

THE COLD CALL

This section explains how to make a COLD CALL.

Introduction

The cold call is your initial contact with the prospect, typically when you are canvassing a neighborhood or talking with a builder. This call is made without an appointment.

Objectives

- Generate a desire in the prospects to have more versatile, easy to use and water conserving sprinkler system than they had been planning. Cause your prospects to visualize how a properly installed irrigation system will enhance their home and bring out the best features of their home and lot.

- Educate your prospects in all the ways that ABC Irrigation is better than other irrigation companies.

- Set up an appointment for a meeting with both Mr. and Mrs. Homeowner or their builder or landscape architect in the near future.

Tone of the call

- Structured

  — Keep this call brief—approximately 3-4 minutes.

  — Organize this call by using the prepared statements under Steps to Follow During the Call.

  — Don't take up a lot of the prospect's time. Remember, you don't have an appointment.

  — If the prospect invites you in, continue this meeting by using the first appointment call techniques.

- Professional

  — Of course, you should be wearing the appropriate attire whenever you are with a prospect or customer.

Steps to follow

1. Make an initial benefit statement.

   — During the call introduce yourself and ABC Irrigation with the sample opening statement below. You should memorize this statement. Don't wing it on this important first contact with your prospect.

Sample Opening Statement:

> "Hello. I'm _____ from ABC Irrigation and I'm wondering if I could take a minute of your time to tell you how we've been able to help new home buyers such as yourselves with their irrigation needs?"

2. Wait for a response to your question.

— The response may include some objections or misconceptions. Suggested answers are given in the section "Common Objections" and should be studied carefully.

— When you get a positive response to your "opening statement,"

3. Explain how ABC Irrigation is different by saying something like this:

> "There are a number of items that make us different from 95% of the irrigators that may knock on your door. We've been in business for 25 years, and we can provide all the services you may need, from design through final installation. We do all this with in-house employees. We have our own designer that uses the latest state-of-the-art CAD system. We do all the planting and irrigation. We even service our jobs that we install. And remember these are all in-house employees. That means that no subcontractor will set foot on your property. It also means that we are able to control scheduling and quality while keeping the cost down by eliminating middle men. If this sounds like the kind of company you would like to have do your landscape and irrigation, I'd like to make an appointment to come back and discuss your requirements."

4. Wait for a response. Handle any objections.

5. Close the call. Make an appointment for your next meeting.

— Leave a brochure.

NOTE: Never hand out a brochure until you are ready to leave. You want the homeowners to be focused on what you are saying. Giving them anything to look at before you are finished will distract them.

STEPS TO FOLLOW FOR THE COLD CALL

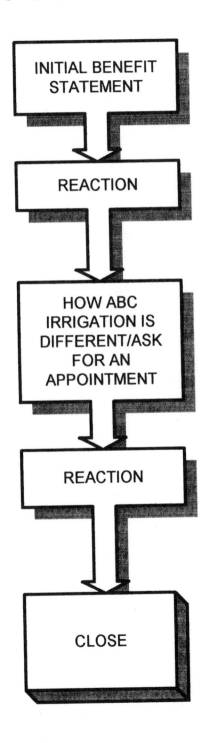

THE FIRST APPOINTMENT CALL

This section explains how to conduct any sales call made by appointment and prior to the closing call.

Introduction

This call includes all meetings with the prospect, set up by appointment, for the purpose of gathering information, determining his or her desires, etc. Almost all of your selling takes place during this call. All calls made after the cold call and prior to the actual presentation of the proposal are included in this category. During this call, both Mr. and Mrs. Homeowner should be present or whoever the decision maker is in the case of builders.

Objectives

- Create a desire in your prospects to have ABC Irrigation do their irrigation.

- Discover their decision-making process.

  — How will they decide?

  — Who will decide?

- Determine their budget.

- Determine their *specific* requirements. Find out if a sprinkler system is a "must" or "would be nice." Ask if your competition is a vacation cruise or another contractor. Suggest that they are making an invaluable investment and that they will be able to reap the rewards for years to come.

- Sell them an irrigation plan, if applicable.

Tone of the call

- Rapport-building.

- Information-gathering.

  — Listen carefully so that you get the facts straight.

  — Be sensitive to their requirements.

- Well organized, but less structured than the cold call.

Steps to follow

1. Start with an ice breaker and continue with no more than 5 minutes of small talk. Comments such as:

   "This is a nice tract. How did you happen to move here?"

   "What kind of work do you (both) do ?"

   These are good ways to build rapport.

2. State your agenda with a statement such as, "Here's what I'd like to do tonight. I'd like to briefly tell you about our company, and then spend most of our time defining your requirements."

3. Explain who you are: introduce ABC Irrigation using the sales kit, spend no more than 10 minutes telling them about ABC Irrigation. Be alert to things that are important to them so that you can key in on them later.

4. Define their requirements.

    - Using sample plans and pictures from your sales kit, begin to discuss and define their desires.

    - Ask open-ended questions to get the most information. For example, "What other types of irrigation systems have you had installed before?" (Start your questions with who, what, when, why, how because they cannot be answered with a "yes" or "no.")

For example:

    - "How soon would you like the job done?"

    - "What's important to you? Ease of maintenance? Saving water?"

    - "What overall look do you want?"

    - "What do you expect of ABC Irrigation?"

    - "What other types of systems have you had installed before?"

    - "What did you like or dislike about them?"

    - "How much are you planning to spend?"

    - "What do I need to do for you to choose ABC Irrigation?"

    - "What will it take for you to feel the job is a success?"

      NOTE: Think of all the valuable information you can get from this last question!!

59

Answers to these questions are extremely valuable. They let you know what's important to your prospect. Use these answers later as a statement of their requirements that you will be meeting.

- Listen carefully and then restate their response. This shows them that you understand their requirements and gives them a chance to correct you if you don't.

5. Sell an irrigation plan. (If applicable)

Once their requirements are well defined, explain that the best approach is to finalize those requirements in the form of an irrigation plan.

Explain why this is so, the cost of such a plan, and what the plan will include. Show them a sample plan.

6. Close the call when you feel you've exchanged all the necessary information.

- Be affirmative, excited and assumptive. (e.g. "I understand what you want.")

- State their desires as a fact. ("This is going to look great!")

- Express your conviction that ABC Irrigation can do what they want.

- Be specific on what is going to happen (e.g. "You will have a plan drawn and a written proposal") And when these things will happen. ("I will be calling you within the next 3 days...")

- Convince your prospects of the benefit of the

next meeting so they will be looking forward to it.

- If appropriate, get a conditional commitment with a question like, "If I can do all the things we've discussed and stay within your budget, is there any reason why you wouldn't do business with ABC Irrigation?" If possible, don't leave until they make some kind of response. This is called getting a conditional commitment. They need to get used to saying yes to you.

KEY: This is their last chance to state additional requirements so that when you return with the proposal there will be no surprises.

STEPS TO FOLLOW FOR THE FIRST
APPOINTMENT CALL

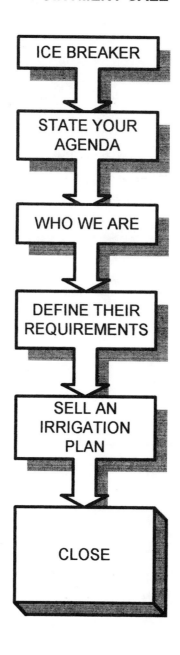

ICE BREAKER

STATE YOUR AGENDA

WHO WE ARE

DEFINE THEIR REQUIREMENTS

SELL AN IRRIGATION PLAN

CLOSE

THE CLOSING CALL

This section explains the sales procedure of getting a signed contract from your prospect.

Introduction

This is your final meeting with the prospect. At this meeting, you present the irrigation plan and go over your proposal. At the end of your presentation, the prospect should sign the contract. This call should be straightforward, matter-of-fact and without surprises. No new information or requirements should surface from your prospect. Similarly, everything in the irrigation plan, the proposal, and about ABC Irrigation should be just what they expected based on your previous conversations. If new information or requirements do surface at this time, evaluate your previous appointment call(s) to determine why. Understanding why all the necessary information wasn't brought out earlier will help you avoid this kind of problem in the future.

Objectives

- Secure a signed contract.

- Secure a deposit.

- Convince your customers that they have been given a fair deal, have chosen the right company, and will enjoy a terrific finished product.

Tone of the call

It is important for you to communicate the following qualities because they are contagious and you want your prospects to catch them.

- Enthusiasm. This is probably the most important — be sure to project this quality.

- Confidence.

- Expectancy.

Steps to follow

1. Open the conversation with an enthusiastic (during the call) statement like:

   "We've got it all for you — a plan that meets your needs and fits your budget."

   "We've come up with just what you wanted."

2. Restate their requirements.

   The best way to do this is roll out their irrigation plan and point out the special features that are important to them that you have been careful to include. Doing this shows that you are meeting the requirements they stated during your previous call(s).

3. Get their reaction and answer any questions.

4. Review the cover letter with them.

5. Review the proposal.

6. Close the call by having them sign the contract and give you a deposit.

   For example:

   — I will need your authorization signature and a deposit check in order to reserve a place on our construction calendar.

— What is your preference for the controller location?

— When would you like for us to get started?

— I will need your initials on pages one and two and both (husband and wife) of your signatures on page three.

— Where would you like us to drop the materials?

— Our hours of operation are Monday through Friday, 7:00 a.m. to 5:00 p.m. Will that work with your schedule?

— I feel as if we are very close to consummating this contract, how about if I throw in a drip system for your hanging baskets to sweeten the deal?

— Outline future events and leave the construction schedule with them.

— Explain that you will call them with specific dates.

STEPS TO FOLLOW FOR
THE CLOSING CALL

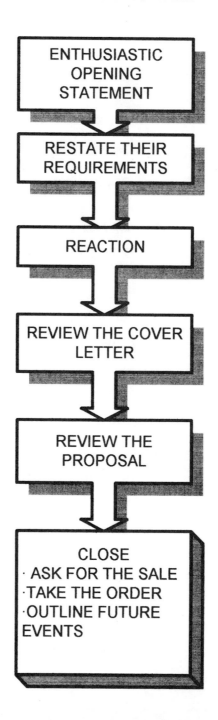

ENTHUSIASTIC
OPENING
STATEMENT

RESTATE THEIR
REQUIREMENTS

REACTION

REVIEW THE COVER
LETTER

REVIEW THE
PROPOSAL

CLOSE
· ASK FOR THE SALE
·TAKE THE ORDER
·OUTLINE FUTURE
EVENTS

SPECIAL SITUATIONS

This section explains how to handle certain situations that occur from time to time.

Particular situation

The telephone call requesting a irrigation bid. This is similar to a cold call.

Procedure

1. Be enthusiastic and thankful for this opportunity to bid the job.

2. Don't bore the prospect with a sales pitch over the telephone.

3. Set up an appointment.

4. Handle the appointment as you would any first appointment.

Particular situation

A request to bid existing irrigation plans drawn by the prospect's architect or by a competing irrigation company.

Procedure

1. Determine whether your prospect has received other bids already.

   If he/she has, find out what he/she doesn't like about those bids (e.g., why he/she hasn't committed to one of them).

- If price has been the problem, indicate that your price probably won't vary greatly from the others.

- Find out what he/she wants to spend and offer to bid his/her plan, making any modifications necessary to do the job for his/her price. Don't ruin your reputation by cutting your price.

- If he/she agrees to this, take the time to develop a relationship with him/her, explaining the many benefits of doing business with ABC Irrigation.

  NOTE: Don't get into a price-only situation with the prospect. Remember if he/she has a relationship with someone else, he/she will probably be willing to pay a few more dollars to do business with them.

2. If the prospect has not received other bids, do everything you would do in a first appointment call except defining his/her plan requirements and selling a plan. For example:

- Sell ABC Irrigation and the added value of doing business with you.

- Develop rapport.

- Find out the specific things that are important to him/her (e.g. His/her hot button, what's going to make him/her buy from you). (See questions to ask in Step 11 under Probe.)

COMMON OBJECTIONS

This section presents the most common objections you will encounter during a sales call and suggests some answers. You should familiarize yourself with these objections now so that they will not throw you off balance during an actual call.

Remember, by voicing their objections, the prospect gives you valuable information that can be used to your advantage if handled correctly. They expect you to argue with them, so soften your response by showing that you understand their concern, but do not agree with the objection. A good way to begin your response is, "I can appreciate (or understand) your concern...." Before you attempt to answer his objection, be sure that you do understand it.

After you have answered, get back on track with the rest of your sales call.

Sample objections and sample responses to the COLD CALL

1. *"We'll probably use the XYZ company."*

   "I can understand that it would be advantageous to have the decision-making process behind you. However, irrigation does represent a major financial investment. I feel it would be in your best interests to get a proposal from a company like ours. So if I could take just a minute of your time to tell you how we're different from most irrigation companies, you might find it helpful."

2. *"I already have two bids."*

   The best response here is the same as the one above. In a situation like this, there is a high probability that even if your prospect lets you bid their job, they won't use you unless your price is much lower than either of the two companies that they are entertaining. Be sensitive to this probability so that you won't waste a lot of time.

If you should get your foot in the door, try to identify areas of dissatisfaction, e.g., the price, the irrigation plan, the company's performance. Focus on satisfying those particular areas in order to set yourself apart from the competition.

3. *"We won't be doing our sprinklers for six months."*

"I can appreciate that. Sprinklers are a major decision and investment. Many of my customers have found it helpful to get the planning done early so that when the time is right for sprinklers, they'll be ready. I'd like to meet with you at your convenience to define your requirements and prepare an irrigation plan. Then you'll know what you could install and what it costs."

4. *"I plan to do the sprinklers myself."*

"I can definitely understand that. It would be a chance for some physical exercise and you'd be able to save money. But for a home like this, I feel you would benefit from a professional irrigation design and installation. It has been my experience that when owners much like yourself tackle a sprinkler system, nothing but grief will come from it. With all of the governmental regulators, city inspectors looking for permits and code violations, rock hard ground, having to run back and forth to the home center for parts that you did not figure that you would need, equipment rental and break-downs and what not, it can surely ruin your entire summer. Maybe you should reconsider. I'd like to meet with you, define your requirements, and prepare a plan. Then I'd be glad to bid some of the more difficult items — such as the sprinkler system, drain lines, and soil preparation — so that it would be all ready for you to do the enjoyable part, the planting."

5. *"I'm too busy to discuss sprinklers right now."*

"I can appreciate that, and it was not my intent to get into a long conversation with you now. What I did want to do is introduce myself and make an appointment to come back at your convenience and discuss your irrigation needs. Is that something you'd be interested in?"

Common objections and responses to the first appointment call

1. *"Why should I have to pay for an irrigation plan?"*

"Well, please understand that a good plan saves money in the long run because every contingency has been planned for. As in any project, you need to start with a good design, so I feel that the cost really represents a wise investment. Also, when we do the actual irrigation work for you, we'll deduct the cost of the plan from our proposal."

2. *"I would rather not tell you what my budget is."*

"I can appreciate that, but I really need to have a

price range to give to the designer so that your plan will be drawn in accordance with your budget. Certainly it would be counterproductive for me to come back here with a plan and a proposal much higher than your expectations. If you could give me a price range, I could have the plan designed accordingly."

3. *"We'll want to get other bids so we won't be committed to you when you come back with a plan and a proposal."*

"I can understand that, but I think that you will find our price and the services we offer might be so attractive that you might decide you don't need other bids. What are the key factors on which you will make your buying decision?" Or, "If all your bids were identical in price, what would be your selection criteria?"

Sample objections and suggested responses to the closing call

1. *"We want to get another bid because..."* (the suggested responses to the sentence might be completed with either *"Your price is higher than I expected"* or with *"The plan looks skimpy for that price."*) In either case, proceed as follows:

   NOTE: If the prospect's requirements and budget are properly defined during the first appointment call, you shouldn't encounter this objection.

   At this point, do all you can to satisfy them (modify the plan, etc.) and to keep them from getting a bid with another contractor.

If they insist on another bid, encourage them to be sure that the other company bids the plan exactly as you did and gives him a detailed cost breakdown. Stress again the added value (which hopefully you have conveyed to him during previous calls) of doing business with ABC Irrigation. Encourage them to be sure that a competitor can and will provide the same services as you are providing.

After you have made these points, continue with: "We've spent a lot of time together, and I wonder if you would give me the opportunity to meet with you again after you receive another bid to see where we stand."

Close the call with the understanding that you *will* call him.

2. *"You can't start when I want you to."*

"Mr.____ , there's nothing I would like better than to start this job on the date you requested. But we schedule and manage our resources very efficiently, and once we start a job we stay on it until it's done.

So I can't pull anyone off another job to start yours right away. However, once we start your job, it will progress rapidly. I don't know of any company that starts and finishes a job as quickly as we do. So I believe that if you wait for us, your job will be done by the same time another company might do it if they started tomorrow! And, when we do your irrigation, work will progress with a lot less interruptions. Does that sound reasonable?"

3. *"We're waiting for financing."*

> "I can certainly understand that. Is that the only thing that's keeping you from committing to this project?"

> Or you could offer an alternative financing package at far more attractive rates. This could be very conducive to signing, especially if you do all of the leg work to the loan officer. The less reasons not to use you the better.

> If the prospect indicates that financing is the remaining hurdle, encourage them to sign the contract anyway so that you can get their project scheduled with the understanding that the agreement is contingent on them securing financing.

GENERAL SALES TECHNIQUES OVERVIEW

This section presents several sales techniques that apply to any situation. Mastering these concepts and approaches will help develop your selling skills.

FEAR, UNCERTAINTY AND DOUBT

This section explains how to overcome these negative attitudes in your prospect.

Introduction

Fear, Uncertainty and Doubt — the *FUD'S* — block decision making. Present yourself in a knowledgeable, professional light to build your prospect's confidence in you and to help eliminate the *FUD'S* . Always be positive and aggressive, stressing all the advantages of doing business with ABC Irrigation that apply to his concerns. As a good salesperson, you should be alert to the *FUD'S* and remove these stumbling blocks by stressing the following facts about yourself and your company.

Points to remember

- We have the best resources and you represent the best company (e.g. ABC Irrigation is different and better).

- We can perform (e.g. ABC Irrigation has a track record).

- Every person in this organization is well trained to do his task.

- We are organized to ensure smooth progress of this job (e.g. Excellent field supervision, project planning, etc.).

- You can provide them with previous client references to reassure them that they will be totally satisfied with ABC Irrigation.

SELL ADVANTAGES, NOT FEATURES

This section discusses perhaps the most common mistakes sales people make and explains how to avoid them.

Introduction

In presenting their product or service, most sales people focus on the features. But the fact is that people don't buy features, they buy advantages. If your prospect can say, "So what? What does that feature mean to me?" then you are not adequately presenting the advantages of your product or service.

Definitions

- A feature states a fact about a product or service. e.g. "We install riser pipes with swing joints."

- An advantage explains the *value* of the feature to the prospect. e.g. "Every sprinkler is fitted with swing joints which greatly reduce the chances of breaking the riser if it is hit by the lawn mower or a car tire." Or, "Paying for wasted water and the cost of unnecessary service calls."

Sales procedure

1. State the feature.

2. Explain the advantage.

3. Get your prospect's reaction. e.g. Ask "Is this important to you? Is this what you would want?"

4. Adjust your presentation to focus on what *is* important to your prospect.

THE TRIAL CLOSE

This section explains how and when to use the trial close.

Introduction

A trial close is a valuable sales technique. It may be used during any interaction with a prospect, but probably is most effectively used during the first appointment call.

What the trial close accomplishes

- Reveals what your prospect is thinking and where you really stand.

- Tells you if the prospect is ready to buy.

- Gets the prospect into the decision making mode.

- Encourages the prospect to make some small decisions, and doing that will make it easier for him to make the final decision.

How to handle this call

- Ask open-ended questions to allow them to express themselves. e.g., "How does that sound?"

- Be positive and assumptive — use "us," "we," etc. e.g., "Here's how *we'll* do that."

- Ask questions that have to be answered with a "Yes." This keeps the tone positive.

Summary: Making calls in person is a fact in the contracting world. There is no substitute for a face behind the voice to add a personal touch. This business is based on relationships.

✔ ACTION PLAN

Develop and rehearse a distinct sales pitch. Study this part until you thoroughly and completely understand how all the parts work together.

NOTES

STEP 11

BUILDING THE SALE

When it comes to acquiring new customers, I probably have tried just about every possibility. It has been my experience that by taking baby steps and trying different ideas as I went along, I was able to find out which ideas brought the most benefit. I remember once interviewing a marketing specialist and one of his comments was, "The rule of thumb is, people in business should allocate 7-10% of their revenue for sales and marketing." I don't know if this "rule of thumb" holds true today or not. The reality is, without sales and marketing efforts there would be no need for you to install sprinklers or do winter servicing.

I know what you are thinking, "Man alive! If I had 7-10% in this project I wouldn't spend it on advertising, I'd go and buy me that new Bass boat." You will find that as your business volume grows and the profits increase, the money will become available to experiment on some other means of marketing. Try to take things slowly and track how much each type of marketing costs and if you are receiving the desired results. (Please see sample chart on page 111 for tracking calls). This way, it won't overwhelm you. Certain items that you will be purchasing for marketing will be amortized over a long period of time even though you pay for it all up front. For example, when you purchase five hundred brochures and you receive a bill for a couple of thousand dollars, try to keep in mind that this includes the art work, layout, printing, etc. Besides that, try to visualize how long it would take to either mail or hand deliver five hundred brochures. Can you imagine all of the calls you would get then?

The following is a suggested list of items that you should *or* could be doing to generate more prospects or help you close the deal.

1. Following up on all referrals and leads, no matter how big or small. If the job is too small, you should have a relationship with a smaller contractor that you can refer the job to possibly for a finder's fee. Or, you can sign the job up yourself and subcontract the work. In the event the job is too large and clearly out of your league, *do not* tackle this with your crews. I recommend working your way up to larger jobs so that your experience level and crew size will fit accordingly. Trying to subcontract out the work to a larger contractor could work, but I would discourage it.

2. Ask your current clients for referrals of someone that could use your services. You would be surprised as to the response. A lead or referral by a friend, neighbor or fellow purchasing agent is far superior than digging one up on your own. (Please see follow-up survey in Continued Communication).

3. Ask your client to write you an endorsement on their letterhead, preferably corporate letterhead. Having numerous testimonials ready for your prospective client gives them the feeling that someone else has already taken the gamble in hiring you, thus lowering their risk mentally. This will add tremendous credibility and will lower their apprehension. As I was ready to close a sale, I would make one small concession in return for a favorable testimony. Provided, of course, that my firm performed to their standards.

4. Have a written warranty that is longer than the industry standard. As time goes on, competition continues to

grow and the stakes get higher and higher, this is one item I found helps close a lot of deals. If everyone else offers a 1 year warranty on the sprinkler system, try 2 years. Whatever your angle, make sure you count the costs before you make the commitment.

5. Tell a story about you and your organization when you advertise. People are hungry for interesting details. These could include: Yellow Pages, newspapers, lead generating fliers, radio, TV. Unless you received an "A" in high school creative writing, you may consider hiring advertising professionals that specialize in writing ad copy.

Robin's Law: Always test and track your mediums for advertising. This will allow you to find out what works best and which gives you the best return for your invested dollar.

---

6. Utilizing direct mail marketing. However, you must be specific about your target group. With today's sophisticated means of tracking peoples buying habits, you can pinpoint just about anyone.

7. Telemarketing. It has been my experience that telemarketing has borne little fruit in this industry. One way of utilizing it could be by sending out a mailer and then a follow up call as a lead generator for your sales staff. Remember, you can't sell over the phone. If your experience has been different, great.

8. Running special events like an Open House to disseminate information. This is an excellent way of capturing peoples names and addresses that are truly interested. It also is effective with other trade related professionals like landscape architects, builders, etc. The down side is it is very expensive to advertise and set it up.

9. Use of your trade memberships to your advantage. Most organizations have an awards program. Entering your projects and winning a plaque or trophy will allow you to demonstrate to the customer why you might be more valuable than the competition. With certain clients, you will be appealing to their egos. Besides that, everyone likes to believe that they are hiring an award winning contractor. Some examples could be the Building Industry Association, MAME, Gold Nugget, or your local chapter of the landscape or irrigation association.

10. Developing a quality control program. Make up a check list for finish details to insure that your crews are paying attention to all of the minute parts. Making the form in 2 part NCR (no carbon required) will allow you to put one in the client master file and have one to send them at the completion of the job. This too is a tremendous tool for helping close the contract. Along the same lines is including an irrigation service manual. This manual should include suggested watering schedules including new lawn establishment, seasonal adjustments, etc., how to maintain the sprinklers on a regular basis, and a complete timer operator's manual, names and telephone numbers for any warranty work.

Prospecting for new clients needs to be done everyday

Prospecting for new clients needs to be done every day. This can be equated to a treasure hunt. In order to find the golden egg, an exhaustive search needs to be performed by leaving no stone unturned looking for business. Some different ways to do this are by utilizing referrals from friends or past customers. Or, you can join breakfast clubs, Rotary, Lions and the like, professional associations, Board of Realtors, architects, churches. Use mailers/ brochures that can be sent to lawyers or doctors. You may want to consider ads in magazines, Yellow Pages, or going door-to-door which is probably the most effective for individual residences. Utilizing door hangers is an effective way to generate residential leads. However, this industry is built on personal contact and there is nothing like meeting your client face-to-face and building a relationship. This applies whether it is for homeowners or a purchasing agent for a builder or developer.

In the past few decades the cycle time of initial contact to signed contract has grown. Some experts say it has gone from 3 contacts to 10 or 12 before you get a signed contract. It has been my personal experience that using direct mail marketing to new homeowners, builders or developers for new construction leaves a lot to be desired. It seems by the time the owners receive the first mailing, they have already received numerous propositions from the local contractors. If you are currently using this method and experiencing marginal results, you may want to start knocking on doors.

I found that after purchasing mailing lists and sending out letters, it was cheaper and more effective to go door to door or hire competent salespeople. It turned out that people like to associate a face with a voice and a company. Your personality is part of what you are selling. Besides, the other contractors are going to get the jump on you if you choose not to canvas personally.

YOUR IMAGE TO THE CUSTOMER

1. First impression goes a long way and will dispel any assumptions that people may have made about you prior to your arrival. Dress professionally. No shorts, boots, tank tops. Ties may be an option depending on the clientele. Doctors, lawyers and accountants prefer this attire. For some others, a button down or golf shirt is

acceptable. Make sure your hair is combed and you exercise personal hygiene. Shoes clean, walk with confidence, project authority, and always a firm hand shake. This projects success and that you are highly professional. If it is for a homeowner, *never* park on their driveway.

2. Depth of knowledge. This pertains to how well you know irrigation. Irrigators not only need to know hydraulics, it is very beneficial to understand the relationships between soil, water and plants. You should demonstrate knowledge in both horticulture and hydraulics. For the horticultural novice, there are plenty of books and videos that will help you get acquainted. People are extremely sophisticated today so you had better know the difference between schedule 40 PVC and class 200 or a digital clock versus a mechanical. You must know who your competitors are and how they stack up to your operation. These are your strengths.

3. Breadth of knowledge. This is how well you can converse with others on different topics. The more you read and do, the better you will be able to relate to your clients and their experiences.

4. Flexibility. This is the ability to adapt to other peoples needs.

5. Enthusiasm. You must try to be enthusiastic about your job. I understand that this is not always possible. You must clear your mind and focus on the meeting at hand. You must come across as genuinely interested.

PREPARATION AND WARM UP

Problem: People basically do not trust contractors. Due to various elements throughout the decades, this industry as

You should demonstrate knowledge in both horticulture and hydraulics

a whole has developed a bad reputation. The customer's apprehension is very high and their trust is very low. In order for you to be successful at closing the deal, these two items need to be reversed to a point where the trust is high and the apprehension is very low. This is not done easily. Trust needs to be built and earned. ***Start off by being on time for your appointment.*** Then, start talking about them. Where are they from, and did they like the last location? Do they have kids, family? What is the same and/or different about this place? Do they entertain? etc. Again, I can't emphasize the importance of being genuine. In this day of every one trying to get into sales, everyone is getting some sort of training on trying to get to know people. The problem is that the client picks up on the fact that you are trying to sell, so you have to be genuine in your interest for them.

PROBE

What is it that they want, why, can they afford it? I prefer that you use the word *invest* when it comes to talking about money. This is the place to ask open ended questions. You know, the who, what, where, when, why, and how questions. The idea is to pull information out of them. The majority of purchases are based on emotion. The balance are based purely on need. Ask them about a budget. Some will say unlimited, others will give some unrealistic low number. I've found that the majority will not commit and would like for you to tell them. The problem here is that they do know how much they are willing to spend, but are unwilling to divulge this information. Their concern is that if they say how much, you will use up every bit of that amount and then some, if given the chance. The reality is that you need to know their budget if you are to design something that will work for them. You need to explain this to them.

Trust needs to be built and earned

The majority of purchases are based on emotion

Ask the *questions* that no one else will. Too many contractors find themselves or their sales people filling out sales reports on people who virtually do not have an interest in having work done in the immediate future. A few of these questions will help you pre-qualify the client so that you are not dealing with a tire-kicker. I'm sure that you have a list of your own questions that work as well.

- When is the job going to be installed?

- When would you like for us to do the work?

- How long do you plan to live in this home?

- Is this your first sprinkler system?

- If no, what did you like/dislike about prior systems?

- Are you planning future landscape changes?

- What kind of electric appliances do you have in the kitchen? (So you can determine if the client prefers digital push buttons or mechanical dials for their controllers.)

Once you establish that they are a real buyer, move on to the next couple of questions that will help you lay the ground work for what is really important to your buyer. You will have to come out and ask them, "What type of things are important to you?"

1. Price?

2. Workmanship?

3. Reliability?

4. Warranty?

5. Water usage efficiency?

Then you need to ask how they would rank them in order of importance. Most people will start off with saying that they are cost conscious. Then they might say that a good, comprehensive warranty is important. Then your people should be reliable and their workmanship must be tops and to round it off they will have to perform like triathletes!

My recommendation is to ask the client questions that will help determine which of these items is more important than the other. I prefer to ask questions that are at opposite ends of the feasibility spectrum. Such as "If I give you a low price, is it okay if we zone the flower beds with the lawn?." Or, "My guys are the best craftsmen around but it will require a great deal of hand digging to avoid damaging your landscaping. They will probably take several extra days to complete your job, is that all right with you?"

What I'm getting at is that through the proper probing, people will find that they will probably be rating the items listed in 1-5 (from above) in a totally different order. More likely the customer will rank workmanship at the top of the list of priorities and cost will become insignificant. The reason being is that he or she likes to feel that they are receiving the best workmanship utilizing the best materials. They will come to the conclusion that you will be giving them these and it will cost X. X may be more than they envisioned, but to them it will all be worth it. This does not mean that you will able to gouge your customer because the order is changed, but they will see that you are educating them on the real facts of your industry. These being that quality, performance and all of the rest cost money. If they feel that they can get your top notch level of service at rock bottom prices, than you might as well cut them loose and let them go and purchase from someone else.

It has been my experience that once the customer gets financially committed, the likelihood of closing the irrigation contract increases tenfold

Sell them a plan for the design that you are about to do for them if the particular situation demands it. It has been my experience that once the customer gets financially committed, the likelihood of closing the landscape contract increases tenfold. Yeah, I know what you are going to say, "The other guys do the plans for free." Well you get what you pay for. The plan is used as a pre-qualifier. If you can't sell a plan, maybe you had better hire a salesperson to do the selling for you. SEE STEP 13 ON HOW TO SET UP A SALES STAFF. The question will arise as to who owns the plan. The homeowner does. It is *their* money. Having you as their contractor should be a pleasurable experience. Producing a plan will help them visualize what is going to take place soon. Having it colored up will make it all that more exciting. Do a one page preliminary plan that will encompass all items discussed, desired and is affordable.

One of the things that worked successfully for me was that the design package was like a shopping list. There was one price for the basic colored rendering that we could work from in the field. Then add-on items like a planting plan, elevation drawing or details of a wood overhead structure, etc., increased by X dollars. Meaning, once the people see all the things they can have for one big price, they almost never bite. However, when you can offer them something psychologically in their budget range, they will buy. After that *they* will add, add, add! This same concept applies to selling a construction project. Start in their affordable range and the people will sell themselves on the things that they have to have.

> *Robin's Law: You can always sell up, you can never sell down. So start mid-range and work your way up.*

Try not to make the plan a concept. If you sell it as such, and I definitely understand the idea behind this, it will come to haunt you. Today people are on the job at 6:30 in the morning with their tape measure checking sprinkler heads for proper spacing and placement. If the plan has too many loose ends, trust will be eroded, your credibility will go down the tubes and you can kiss your referral for doing the neighbor's house goodbye.

PRESENTATION

Prior to meeting with the client, you need to rehearse in your head or with someone else what you plan to say. I found it to be very effective to sit in the car for five or ten minutes before going inside, and role play all of the possible scenarios. These should include any possible questions as well as how you should respond. Don't expect to make the sale, but be prepared for it. You should never smoke or drink while making a presentation of any kind. I remember having a beautiful colored rendering when I knocked over a soda and ruined the plan and the presentation. Some mistakes can be costly. Lay out the plan and try to sit near them so that you can walk them through the site and all of the things they imagined. I am of the opinion that only 5% of clients can visualize accurately how the drawing will transform their yard. It will pay to go slow and explain in great detail. Usually, when the colored rendering is in front of them, they will be impressed. One of the things you need to do as a contractor is to elevate yourself above the rest so you can be distinguished as a professional. Yellow pads and boots don't cut it. During the presentation there might be a change or two. If you look back to the probing stage, this is where detailed notes have to be taken and transferred to your irrigation designer precisely. I used to give my designer notes and when he got the plan roughed out, I would swing

It will pay to go slow and explain in great detail

by his office and check it for accuracy. Sometimes the client needs to be reminded as to what their original requirements were. In the event of large changes, go back to the irrigation designer. If there are small or minor discrepancies, these usually will not present a problem prior to closing of the contract.

DESIRE

As you are doing your presentation and walking them through the different phases of the job, and embellishing on the fantastic job your firm is going to do for them, you are building desire. They are desiring and visualizing you doing all of the things you are speaking about. Make sure you use plenty of adjectives so that they are getting a clear picture of what is about to take place. This brings me to *FAB*, which stands for *Feature*, *Advantage*, and *Benefit*.

People do not buy features, they buy benefits. Selling the feature is just the first step of the process. If they can say, "So what?" to the feature, you have not sold anything. You can start with a *Feature* like "All of your lawn sprinklers will be four inch pop-ups with pressure-activated seals and self retracting nozzles." But then you need to explain the *Advantage* of using this product and then go on to the long term *Benefit* from using the product. By not expanding on the features you are leaving your client in the dark and making you sound shallow, possibly like the competition. Do not hesitate to use different terminology on different items. Remember, this is probably the first time they have heard the terms so make sure the customer stays with you.

THE CLOSE

This is the shortest phase of the sales cycle. If for some reason the customer starts asking questions about your firm

People do not buy features, they buy benefits

or some other out of place question, you probably did not do a thorough job of educating them in the early stages. The customer at this time offers the buying signal.

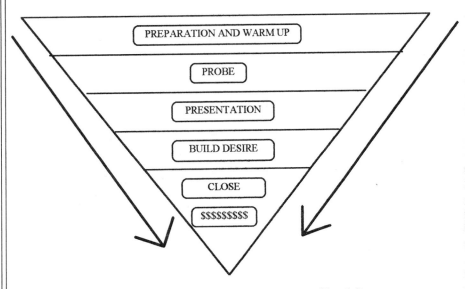

| PREPARATION AND WARM UP |
| PROBE |
| PRESENTATION |
| BUILD DESIRE |
| CLOSE |
| $$$$$$$$$$ |

This diagram briefly shows the direction of building the sale. Most of your time is going to be spent on the top and slowly working your way down to the close. The close should take the least amount of time provided that you did your job correctly in the beginning stages. For practical purposes, the close is the logical conclusion.

There are numerous closing lines and techniques, too numerous to list effectively. In order to be successful, you must ask for the sale. After using the specific verbiage for your particular situation, turn the contract toward them and hand them the pen. It will pay to have the contract filled out prior to your arrival. It is OK to fill in details that are important to them but not be formally addressed, with your pen. Some suggested closing lines are:

- I will need your authorization signature and a deposit check in order to reserve a place on our construction calendar.

- What is your preference for the controller location?

- When would you like for us to get started?

- I will need your initials on pages one and two and both (husband and wife) of your signatures on page three.

- Where would you like us to drop the materials?

- Our hours of operation are Monday through Friday, 7:00 a.m. to 5:00 p.m. Will that work with your schedule?

- I feel as if we are very close to consummating this contract, how about if I throw in ten flats of color to sweeten the deal?

Summary: Building the sale is a methodical way of taking the guess work out of the sales cycle.

✔ ACTION PLAN

Study this area and start rehearsing and practicing on your new clients. The more practice, the better you will become at it.

STEP 12

BUYING SIGNALS

The following is a list of some of the most common verbally-expressed items that your clients will say *or* do when they show a desire for your product or service. I have found that as time goes on during the sales cycle, the customer is getting smarter because of the education that you are giving them. They may ask some of these questions as a desire to fully understand what it will take to do the project.

I encourage you to get to know these buying signals well so that when they are expressed, you will have pen in hand and spring into action by having them sign your contract.

VERBAL BUYING SIGNALS

"When can you get started?"

"How long does a job like this take?"

"Can we finance this project?"

"Do we have to pay cash?"

"What happens if we later decide we want to irrigate the _____ area?"

"What if we change our mind on bed locations?"

"This plan sure looks good!"

"Is this the proper time of year to plant a lawn?"

"Do you personally supervise the work?"

"Will you have to get permits from the building department?"

"How long before I can mow the sod?"

"Does your company offer an annual maintenance contract?"

"How will you install the pipe in the beds around the house?"

"Does the price include tax?"

"Will we be provided instructions on how to take care of our new sprinkler system?"

"Will you provide lien releases?"

"Will you have to use subcontractors?"

"Do you have a foreman that is bilingual?"

"So what's next?"

PHYSICAL BUYING SIGNALS

Client leans forward.

Client appears to relax.

Client looks intently at something on the plan.

Sudden change in attitude.

Summary: The customer's buying signals are the first recognizable actions that they do to let you know that they are ready to make a purchase.

✔ ACTION PLAN

Learn to recognize these signals starting with your next potential deal.

STEP 13

SET UP A SALES STAFF

It is my
recommendation
that you do all
agreements in
writing

In the event that you decide to delegate the responsibility of selling your company's services, you should start with developing and establishing a sales policy. It is imperative that this policy be established prior to hiring anyone. This could be as little as a job description, or consist of a contract that is individually tailored for each salesperson. It is my recommendation that you do all agreements in writing. This will encourage only the best to come to work for you and meanwhile hold you accountable as to what you have committed to them. The following is a proprietary format that was developed and used by me with a great deal of success. You can adapt or modify this as your individual situation dictates.

MARKETING COMPENSATION PROGRAM

Duties and Responsibilities

1. Salesperson shall locate, generate and/or follow up on all leads.

2. He/she shall prepare estimates and present proposals to prospective customers, utilizing a sales assistant*.

3. Salesperson is responsible for collecting all moneys from deposits to final payments. This does not include accounts that are being litigated. All checks will be made payable to ABC Irrigation.

4. Salesperson shall frequently interface with project manager/supervisor during the course of installation to insure customer satisfaction.

5. It is the salesperson's responsibility to check and sign off on all work done by sales assistant. Final responsibility lies with the salesperson.

6. Estimates should be checked by salesperson for possible increased charges, such as site conditions, unusual plant material or paving material, etc.

7. Billing is to be done each week, prior to Wednesday, to insure timely delivery of bills.

8. Other tasks to be handled by salesperson will be customer problem solving, complaints, relations and communication.

* Sales Assistant: This person's job was to design plans and develop a labor and materials list for the salesperson. They received a base salary with 1% and .5% commission for residential and commercial jobs respectively. This allowed the salesperson to access more potential clients in more active communities.

Sales Goals

Each salesperson is expected to meet or exceed the sales goal established for the year. There will be no side jobs, weekend irrigating, etc. This is a conflict of interest and termination will result. All leads, e.g. homeowners, architects, builders, developers, etc., that the salesperson has accumulated become property of ABC Irrigation.

Each salesperson is expected to meet or exceed the sales goal established for the year

COMPENSATION

Salesperson shall be paid 7% commission on all residential business closed, and 2.5% of all commercial business closed. Pricing of jobs is to be done according to ABC Irrigation standard price sheet or off of computer generated proposals. Commission will be paid as sales checks are received, prior to 5:00 p.m. on each Thursday . The salesperson's commission will be paid for that amount on Friday.

Additional incentive programs will be offered periodically for products that need emphasis. Such incentives may be in the form of commission or awards. ABC Irrigation shall provide salesperson with major medical insurance, dependents not included at this time. A $50.00 per month allowance for entertaining clients is provided , with proper receipts. Pagers are also paid for by company.

SUPPLIES

Salesperson shall supply his/her own car and auto insurance with liability equal to $1,000,000 and naming ABC Irrigation as additional insured. The cost above and beyond the salesperson's existing liability cost will be paid by ABC Irrigation, proof will be necessary of insurance coverage and the additional cost. Also, the salesperson shall supply at his/her own expense: gas, pencils and pens, phone at home, tape measure and any other miscellaneous items pertinent to the function of his/her job. ABC Irrigation will supply brochures, photograph portfolio, contracts, business forms, desk, and telephone at our main office.

Salesperson shall be paid 7% commission on all residential business closed, and 2.5% of all commercial business closed

VACATIONS

At this time, vacation shall be limited to two unpaid weeks and should be scheduled one month in advance.

TERRITORY

Salesperson shall have the exclusive right to sell in the area bounded as follows: East of the 23 freeway to the Pine Cone county line, and south to Hibiscus county line. Should territory change during a job in process, relinquishing salesperson shall receive 80% of total commission.

TERMINATION

In the event of voluntary or involuntary termination, moneys due to salesperson will be paid as checks are received by ABC Irrigation, not earlier. Commission will be paid on jobs signed within 10 days following termination.

NOTE: The above terms and conditions are subject to review and modification at management discretion.

I have read this marketing plan, understand it and agree to abide by it.

_____   _____
Salesperson   Date   Owner   Date

Summary: Setting up a sales staff is a sure fire way of multiplying your time and talent.

✔ ACTION PLAN   Develop your sales policy.

HOW TO HIRE A SALESPERSON

Immediate opening for well-groomed, self-motivated individual interested in high earnings and job satisfaction

Now that you have a basic format to keep your salesperson under wraps, now is the time to locate one. Put the word out to people in the industry that you are hiring. If you happen to know of a potential candidate that is currently employed at XYZ firm, tell him/her that you are expanding your operation and were wondering if he/she knows of anybody that might be interested in coming to work for you. This usually puts a subtle bug in their ear and he/she might ask if they can submit their resume.

Another way is to run an ad in the newspaper, trade magazines, local association newsletters or distributor bulletin boards. The magazines can be a problem because of the tremendous lead time. An example of ad copy might read like this:

> IRRIGATION SALES. Immediate opening for well-groomed, self-motivated individual interested in high earnings and job satisfaction. Must have minimum 5 years sales experience in irrigation industry. Come join the irrigation professionals at ABC Irrigation. 123-4567. Ask for Bill.

When the calls start coming in, be ready. Even though the ad was written for industry professionals, you will get calls from people with backgrounds from high school candy sales to shoes or copiers. Some peoples' theory is that they would prefer to make a irrigator into a salesperson rather than salesperson into an irrigator. I've hired both. They both have pros and cons. The problem with hiring a salesperson that has no irrigation savvy, but strong people skills, is that when they are ready to close the deal, a technical question seems to arise and because of their lack of hard knowledge, the deal can unravel. I've found this to be true, on occasion, in the commercial arena.

When you talk to the applicants on the phone, try to qualify them as much as possible. Try to get out of them the specifics of their current and past career. This will help you eliminate the people who want to break into the construction field. I recommend that you let them break in with some other company. For your first salesperson, try to go with someone that has irrigation sales and design experience.

For your first salesperson, try to go with someone that has irrigation sales experience

Have them send a resume so that you can review it prior to the personal interview. Allow 30 minutes minimum for the interview process. Make sure that they are on time. Give them 10 minutes maximum allowance for traffic. You want someone that looks as if they fit your company profile. Your preference should be that he/she is well dressed and groomed properly. Look for someone that is hungry, not greedy, someone with initiative, energy, schooling and above average grades. Hiring a college graduate is preferable. They should come from a family of modest circumstances. If he/she is married, this could be a sign of stability. However, I don't recommend that you ask family questions (this is illegal under current federal law).

SAMPLE SALES INTERVIEW QUESTIONNAIRE

Applicant Name:

Currently Employed? Yes   No

Last 3 jobs:

1 _____ How long? _____

2. _____ How long? _____

3 _____ How long? _____

Salary requirements: _____

(NOTE: for interviewer only): This is an (entry level/advanced) position with much training required and a lot of potential. Pay is commensurate with experience. At this point interview may be terminated due to fact that his/her salary require- ments are too high for your budget. As you go through these questions, listen for answers that will indicate his/her sales experience and maturity. Such as: him/her moving on to larger and better challenges, or by him/her saying that the company was right for him/her at that time. The interviewer needs to look for consistency and direction of the candidate.

What do you know about ABC Irrigation? _____

What type of irrigation experience do you have? _____

Are you a licensed or I.A. Certified designer? _____

Why do you want to work in the irrigation field? _____

What type of sales experience do you have? _____

Why do you want to work in sales? _____

What is your idea of a good salesperson? _____

How many miles do you currently drive a year? _____

What kind of automobile do you drive? _____

What year is it? _____

Do you lease or own it?_____How long?_____

If currently in sales, how many sales calls a day do you make? _____

Do you or have you ever had to stay overnight when traveling?_____

Do you pay your own expenses? _____ Which ones?

Meals	yes	no
Car	yes	no
Gas	yes	no
Hotel	yes	no
Telephone	yes	no

Any other expenses that were paid for? _____

Why did you choose your previous employer? _____

Why did you or do you want to leave your previous employer? _____

(NOTE: for interviewer only) We are now ready to evaluate resourcefulness.

If a potential client says "I already have selected my irrigator, but thanks for stopping by anyway," what would you say or do to change their mind? _____

_____

If the customer said " YOU told me that this bed was supposed to be zoned with the planter by the entry, but it isn't." What would you do? _____

_____

If the customer said, "YOUR COMPANY installed the clock in the wrong location," and you were the one that helped them select that location, what would say or do?

_____

What is more important to you, making the sale or taking care of the customer, even if it means losing the sale? _____

If a customer wanted more sprinkler heads, even though the project had adequate coverage, what would you do? _____

What were some of the toughest sales you have made? _____

How did you manage to close the deal? _____

What if you came to my first sales meeting and the two top salespeople said " You'll never beat my sales." What would you think and what would you do? _____

_____

What if you beat the number one salesperson and he/she said to you, "I'll bet you can't do that again." What would you think and what would you do? _____

_____

(NOTE: for interviewer only) At this point, you as an interviewer are looking for healthy competitiveness. Look for people who convey excitement at the challenge of being number one.

Do you feel comfortable with a canned or organized sales approach? Why or why not? _____

Give me your 5 best closing lines.

_____

_____

_____

_____

_____

What are your strengths? _____

What are your weaknesses? _____ __

What is your biggest failure? _____

What would you call rejection? _____

More background information

Have you ever had your drivers license revoked? _____

Have you ever had your car insurance canceled? _____

Have you been convicted of any moving violations in the last 3 years? _____

Do you have a major credit card? _____

How did you obtain your last three jobs? _____

Why did you leave them? _____

What is your favorite hobby? _____

If you don't get (into or back into sales) what else would you like to do? _____

_____

(NOTE, for interviewer only) Willingness to take risk is a good virtue in a salesperson.

If the choice was yours, would you rather have straight salary, salary plus commission, or straight commission? _____

How much do you think my top salesperson earns each year? _____

What do you think is a big salary? _____

What is your biggest achievement? _____

Closing questions

Do you have typing skills? _____

What type of computer knowledge do you possess? _____

We have had many qualified applicants, what makes you special? _____

Why do you want this job? _____

What type of sales training have you had? _____

Do you have any questions? _____

Personal hygiene and appearance _____

Interviewer: _____ Date _____

Summary: Developing and training a competent sales staff is a laborious task but well worth the investment.

✔ ACTION PLAN

Layout territories and areas to be covered, plan on how you will keep the sales staff supplied with leads, hire one salesperson. Follow up sales calls with tracking form.

WEEKLY SALES REPORT

ABC Irrigation

Salesperson _____

Week Ending _____

Date	Job	Address	Phone	Project $ Value	Approx. Close Days			Probability %	Plans by ?	Contractor
					30	60	90			

STEP 15

THE TELEPHONE AS A TOOL

FACT: You are in the service industry. The minute you lose sight of that, you might as well find something else to do. This business is problem solving every day. My suggestion is to find competent people that like to help people with their problems, and success will follow you.

Answer the telephone courteously. Treat people as you would like to be treated. For example: "Good morning, ABC Irrigation. This is Laura, how may I help you?" Your front line secretaries are the first bit of sales for new clients. The customer's first impression should be a favorable one. When dealing with an existing patron, this is an excellent way of reaffirming that they made a wise choice. This is a favorable way of building a satisfied customer base for future referrals. You must return calls promptly whether they are sales oriented or service oriented. Remember, these people are the life blood of your very existence.

The initial call into your company is when you should use the Prospect Log for first time callers. Remember, this will help you evaluate the effectiveness of any and all of your marketing campaigns.

If you have a small business with limited resources, I advise against "call waiting." I have yet to find someone that doesn't mind being interrupted by that annoying "click-click" while you get the next call. A way around this is to have two telephone lines. Use the secondary line for outgoing calls. This way you won't miss any incoming calls. Or, get the "rotary" or "hunting" feature from the phone com-

You must return calls promptly whether they are sales oriented or service oriented

107

pany. It is a small extra charge but well worth the cost of sounding professional.

When returning a call, make yourself ready to speak by putting away paper work, smile, use the caller's name, speak slowly, be articulate. By all means do not interrupt! Let them speak and listen carefully so that you fully understand the nature of the call. Use courtesy phrases. For example: "Thank you," "Please," etc. Always let the other person hang up first.

If you are returning a call to a place of business, the secretary usually asks the nature of the call. Just ask to have the call returned. Very rarely will you be able to effectively communicate what your message is. The exception is if they utilize a voice mail system.

You cannot sell over the telephone. The telephone is used for appointments only. The more you are in front of the client, the more vague the competitor will become. Besides, you would not want to miss out on something being improperly communicated. Always call and confirm an appointment.

When handling a complaint, there is usually pain or dissatisfaction. Try to anticipate problems your client might be experiencing. Just listen to what the client has to say. Try not to get defensive. Talk softly without emotion. Ask to have him repeat problem for your notes, offer an apology, and ask what would it take to resolve the problem. Be careful with this last offer since some people have a distorted view of being compensated for their grief. Be careful with promises, starting dates, and especially completion dates. Pick a date that gives you plenty of time to finish your other obligations. Never say, "Yes, but..." In today's market with discerning buyers and tight money, customers usually want you to start right away. Never mislead them.

You cannot sell over the telephone. The telephone is used for appointments only

---

Robin's Law: Tell people the truth. It makes it easier to remember your stories .

Telling the truth is very important; it builds tremendous credibility. This is where you need it most. If you lose face before you start, it takes a lot to earn it back. Never be late for an appointment. Try to accurately project what is to take place in the next day's construction schedule. Warn them there may possibly be changes.

Use of a message recording machine can be very handy. But let's face it, nobody likes to talk to them. So, if you must use these little rascals, do it right! Buy a good unit that can take extended messages and is known for its reliability. And by all means, if your client or irrigation supplier leaves a message, promptly call them back. I make it a habit of always leaving a message no matter what. If my call doesn't get returned, they don't deserve my business.

When using a machine, have it pick up after 2 - 3 rings. Have a short but concise message and directions as to how you would like the caller to respond. Make sure that you speak clearly and ask the caller to do the same when they leave their message. It can be a real problem trying to call back a potential client when you can't make out their phone number.

My preference is for you to utilize the telephone company voice mail or computer operated voice mail. Telephone company services are about $20 per month per voice mail box. The computer operated boxes range in price from $60 to several hundred dollars. The beauty is that you can customize different voice mail boxes for the different areas of your company. Press one for sales, two for service, three to leave a message, etc. The advantages:

- People are now used to leaving messages with them.

- They are very dependable.

- These devices make your company sound larger and more professional.

- You have eliminated one task that normally would require a live operator.

Any time you can leverage your time or talent by means of a machine that won't need sick, vacation or Worker's Compensation pay, or dependency on some utility company, do it. By making this one time investment, you will be able to make money for years to come.

Cellular phones are a tremendous tool for staying in touch with your office or clients. They can, however, be an irritant while you are traveling. Crackling, popping, and the constant of getting cut off can be enough to upset the most patient. With their increasing popularity and expanding cell sites, communication is vastly improving as well as the cost to operate them. It is my recommendation to buy a cellular phone well after you have established a true need. Looking "cool" and talking on the freeway is not nearly as important as keeping your hard earned money in your pocket. You can use a lot of quarters before justifying several hundred dollars a month in cell phone bills.

Summary: Being courteous and teaching others in your organization to be courteous is paramount to your ultimate success.

✔ ACTION PLAN

Develop a policy and procedure as to how the telephone is to be handled and how calls will be routed throughout your organization.

New Call Prospect Log (sample)

Prospect Log		How Did You See Our Name?																			Reason for Call		
Date	Name Address/Phone	1	2	3	4	5	6	7	8	9	10	11	12	13	14	15	16	17	18	19	20	New System	Add On	Service

1. Customer Referral
2. Friend/Relative
3. Contractor Referral
4. L/A Referral
5. Job Sign

6. Door Hangar
7. Direct Mail
8. Newspaper Ad
9. Truck
10. Employee

11. Distributor
12. Home Show
13. Mall Show
14. T.V.
15. Radio

16. Billboard
17. Ad Specialty
18. Banker
19. Builder/Developer
20. Yellow Pages

NOTES

STEP 16

THE FAX MACHINE AS A TOOL

There is probably nothing as efficient as the fax machine

When it comes to efficiency, there is probably nothing as efficient as the fax machine. I remember it took me a couple of extra years before I came around to getting off of my Brontosaurus and catching up with technology. There certainly is a cost involved up front, but in the long haul, it is well worth it. Don't scrimp on a cheap one either. If you start using it like I think you will, buying last year's Cost Cutter that is no longer in production will only bring you grief.

At first I purchased a stand alone fax machine. Then I had my office manager program the most commonly called numbers used for obtaining quotes from suppliers, my list of builders and developers and the sort. This was really slick since I no longer had to be put on hold and waste a bunch of time repeating endless lines of various PVC fittings or sprinklers and all their separate nozzle patterns. Yes, I had to have my messages in some type of printed form in order to have it transmitted to my destination of choice. That was a little tough since I'm not real good at typing, but my hand-writing is absolutely atrocious, so I learned how to use the word processor to help me out.

I used the fax for sending bids to my general contrac-tors before the deadlines. I also have used it for having builders okay Change Orders. Use a CHANGE ORDER form for any changes whatsoever. Even if there is no dollar increase or decrease. Example: Changing a 6" brand "X" pop-up for a 6" brand "Y." It seems tedious and time con-

It has been my experience that people in construction need to walk around with a handful of CHANGE ORDER forms because people are always trying to change or add things

suming, but when it comes to getting paid, it is best to have all the necessary documentation so that peoples' memories won't be lost as a way to circumvent their financial obligations. It has been my experience that people in construction need to walk around with a handful of CHANGE ORDER forms because people are always trying to change or add things. I would simply fax them a copy of the cost and other pertinent details requesting a signature prior to our commencing the work and asked them to please fax it back. This way at least you have something signed to insure payment. Whether it is for a homeowner or a builder, remember to make sure all work is authorized.

Robin's Law: Never do any work without a signature of an authorized person. Never!

Don't say that you were never warned. I hate to be the bearer of bad news but those people called "homeowners" and "developers" and the like, that resemble humans and are commonly called "customers" are actually part weasel. As defined in Webster's Dictionary, "small, slender flesh eating mammals." And that is exactly what they will do if given the chance. When it comes to the end of the project, everyone that wanted all of the goodies can no longer remember authorizing them. The fax has saved my hide more than once.

With the invention of computers, they now have little fax machines inside of them. Well, almost. You can make neat little cover sheets with room for your messages and push one button and... PRESTO! It is now in the intended's office without having to first print it up, then stand in the fax machine line, then fax it. Now just type it up and that is all she wrote. If, however, you wish to fax a copy of the newspaper article that mentions which awards you just won from the landscape association to dear ol' Mom, keep the stand alone fax machine handy for such tasks. Don't forget to plug it in to the phone line and unplug it when you are finished. If you don't, when you try sending another message through your computer's fax/modem, you are likely to get an error message and have a heck of a time troubleshooting it. I know I did.

One last point. What if the client says, "I'm busy. Could you please fax me the proposal so I can review it tonight?" Well guess what? If you do, you will probably never see or hear from them again. After you have spent hours and hours of extra effort finding out what their needs are and customizing the proposal to fit them specifically, don't let them use you as a comparison for their uncle Harry or your competition to see if your numbers are in line. Be polite and explain that it is to their advantage for you to thoroughly explain the contents of the proposal and contract. If they insist, insist harder. Tell them it is against company policy. No exceptions. Nobody argues with company policy.

Summary: Utilizing the fax machine will multiply your time and efforts for staying in touch with your suppliers and clients.

✔ ACTION PLAN

Research available models and purchase one that will last. Do not buy the cheapest. You get what you pay for.

SAMPLE ADDENDUM TO CONTRACT (CHANGE ORDER)

DATE: 1/1/95

ABC IRRIGATION   ADDENDUM #_____

ATTENTION:

PROJECT:

SCOPE OF WORK AS FOLLOWS: We hereby propose to furnish all materials and labor to install a 4 valve automatic sprinkler system per the plans and specifications prepared by: _____
Associates. All work to be completed in a manner that is common to the trade.

INCLUSIONS:

EXCLUSIONS:

BID PRICE: $_____

This proposal is good for _____days.

Respectfully submitted,

Dave Jones   _____
Account Executive   Owner Signature   Date

THE COMPUTER AS A TOOL

The computer, much like the fax machine, is a highly specialized and efficient tool. The face of this industry has changed dramatically over the last 10 years. The power of the PC (personal computer) has revolutionized the construction industry and will continue to do so for years to come.

If you bought a computer several years ago and are either using it in a minimal way, such as word processing or not using it at all (like collecting dust), I recommend that you trash it if it is a 286 version or older. It never fails to amaze me how a contractor will go out and spend $25,000 on a new truck, but won't spend $2,500 on a computer. The real advantage of a computer is to help you make the repetitive, boring tasks easier to do and add money to your bottom line by multiplying the amount of tasks an individual can do without hiring more personnel.

The question always comes up, "Do I buy a Macintosh or IBM (PC)?" It has been my experience that if your work is more architectural, use the Mac. I have found the IBM has more business related software. If you have a small office requiring one or two computers, I recommend that you start off with a IBM or IBM clone. The clone is just like the IBM, but manufactured by a smaller firm. If you require multiple terminals due to the size of your office, think of a networked system. This will eliminate the need to exchange floppies between computers. Novell makes an excellent network system.

The real advantage of a computer is to help you make the repetitive, boring tasks easier to do and add money to your bottom line

As a contractor, the computer will allow you to process repetitive letters at a key stroke, track your monthly accounting, do estimates and a plethora of other tasks. My first recommendation is to purchase a 486 DX 33 or 40 with a minimum of 8 Megabytes of RAM and a color monitor. Get a hard disk with a minimum of 340MB of space. The price for this stuff is far to cheap to scrimp. Besides, as your business grows, you will use the space.

As for software, Microsoft now has bundled programs together for one discounted price. This allows you to purchase Word (word processing), Access (data base management), Excel (spreadsheet) and a few others all running in the Windows environment. The beauty is that they are backed by the same manufacturer and the programs can all talk to each other.

When it comes to estimating software, there are several to choose from. There are CAD systems with estimating options, standalone units that run independent from CAD — DOS or Windows based. Most firms offer a demo disc that will enable you to see several of their features, ease of operation, reports generated, etc. Call the companies and ask for at least six referrals. Ask the current users detailed questions.

- How long have they had it in operation?

- What don't they like about the program?

- What is the company support program like?

- How does the program perform differently from what the company salesperson said it would accomplish?

Whether your company is large or small, in order for you to be successful you must be able to account for every penny that goes into the job. The way I look at it, one adding mistake or one line item you forgot to include will cost you hundreds, even thousands of dollars. These software systems are a small price to pay for accuracy. You should look at them as a safety net. For some reason, when contractors start preparing prices, especially in a competitive environment, it appears as if they will cut the price no matter how much money it costs them. A good estimating software program will allow you to identify all of your costs, stick to them and make a profit. Let the other guy take it on the chin and build another monument with his name on it.

Let the other guy take it on the chin and build another monument with his name on it

---

Robin's Law: It's not how much volume you do, but how much you keep at the end of the day!

After you have selected the programs you want, I recommend that you start with one and work with it until you have a comfort level that would enable you to go through a complete estimate several times without making any mistakes. Once you have done this, then it is time to move on to the next one, say "Access" for example. I purchased an after market book on how to use Access. I find that originals from the software maker are cumbersome and hard to use. I selected the ABC's of Microsoft Access by Sybex Publishers. The book was extremely easy to use. I just sat down and started to read it from cover to cover and followed the tutorial on my computer. The nice thing about this particular guide is that if your screen doesn't look like the one in the book, you've probably made a mistake.

If the books are still a bit too much, which is quite normal, there are the videos. Some people learn better visually then by reading. Others are better at reading; others do okay at listening. I guess *those* are the *ones* with a vivid imagination. Again, like anything else, these have their price tag. I look at the videos as an investment in my future. The more knowledge I possess, the more hurdles I can overcome, and the more profitable and valuable I become to my company. Some of the best videos come from Keystone Learning Systems, Provo, Utah.

After you have mastered the estimating program, I advocate learning the word processing program. This will allow you to customize your letters with bold letters, under-lines or just about anything that you can imagine. First, put in all of your standard form letters. These would be: letters of introduction to new clients, cover letters for your propos-als, thank you letters, etc. Later in this guide are a few examples. Once you have entered them into the program, give them a unique name such as INTRO or THANKS that will allow your secretary to use them easily. With your simple instructions, after a contract has been signed, a letter of thanks can go out to the client with a minimal amount of work. Now your typewriter will be gathering dust.

Robin's Law: Work smarter, not harder!

. If you have several clients that need to be notified of an event that requires the same letter, most word processing programs have a feature known as Mail Merge. This allows you to build a database with your customers name, address, etc. and send them the same letter without having to do a lot of work. The Mail Merge feature does work very well. However, when it comes to data base management, it has been my experience that these word processing programs have their limitations.

For mass mailings to existing or potential customers, my favorite is the Microsoft Access. With this data base program, the sky is the limit on what you can keep track of with your clients. I found it much easier to print mailing labels by using the query (which is a fancy way of asking your computer to generate a list for you from the data base).

Once you get a handle on the programs and their capacities, you will be capable of multiplying your office staff time and efficiency. At one point in time, my operation had one office person handling the chores of four separate people. And that was without putting in any overtime! You do the math. It doesn't take a brain surgeon to figure out by the end of one year how much money you just added to your bottom line.

Summary: The computer is here to stay. Quoted from an individual that taught me how to build one, "I believe that the computer is in its infancy. The level of sophistication that the computer is at, is like comparing the old Model T to the cars of today."

✔ ACTION PLAN

Purchase yourself a good PC with Windows and the related software. Again, don't scrimp. Train your staff even if it means having them go to special tutoring classes. Without the proper operating knowledge and implementation program, you will not receive any benefit from the computer.

Sample Contract Form (computer generated)
Irrigation Construction Proposal

ABC IRRIGATION
12345 Rotor Ave.
Any Town, CA 99999
(555) 555-5555 License #11111

PROPOSAL SUBMITTED TO	PHONE	DATE
STREET	JOB NAME	
CITY, STATE, ZIP	JOB LOCATION	

SCHEDULE "A"
SCOPE OF WORK

ABC IRRIGATION shall furnish all labor, materials, equipment, services, and competent supervision incidental thereto, necessary to complete the installation of _____ work in accordance with plans and specifications prepared by_____ with subsequent revisions dated through_____,1995, as initialed by the parties.

Irrigation System $
1 Year System Maintenance $

Total $

(note: for residential jobs without specific plans, be as detailed in this area as possible)

Offer to Purchase
Owner   Date

Acceptance
ABC IRRIGATION   Date

SAMPLE CONTRACT FORM (COMPUTER GENERATED)

IRRIGATION CONSTRUCTION PROPOSAL

SUBMITTED TO   DATE:

JOB NAME:

ADDRESS:

SCOPE OF WORK AS FOLLOWS: We hereby propose to furnish all labor and materials to install an automatic irrigation system and all planting per plans and specifications prepared by: ABC IRRIGATION. All work to be completed in a manner common to the trade. Site to be received in a weed and trash free condition graded to 1/10th of a foot to drain unless otherwise noted.

INCLUSIONS: Irrigation, drip system, sod replacement, 1 year system maintenance

EXCLUSIONS: Planting

TOTAL BID PRICE: $12,000

PAYMENT SCHEDULE: $500 down, with weekly progress payments based on work completed. Balance upon completion.

This proposal is good for ____days.

OFFER TO PURCHASE: ACCEPTANCE:

_____   _____
Owner   ABC Irrigation

_____   _____
Date   Date

NOTES

STEP 18

CONTINUED COMMUNICATION

The following sample letters are some examples of how I was able to make a contact with a client and maintain contact throughout the sales cycle. Whenever I had a conversation of any kind, it would be time for me to send him/her a letter. This method was extremely successful because it allowed me to stay in front of the client in a non-invasive way. Once you develop your own letters, keep a separate file on each client so you won't get conversations crossed. The filing system could be by a hard copy or simply in the computer.

Staying in constant communication before and during the sales cycle is not a one time event. Hopefully you will adopt this new practice for all of your clients. It is most important to stay in contact after the award of the contract. This will apply to individual homeowners, developers and other contractors from whom you derive your business. Two ways of doing this is through the implementation of annual maintenance agreements and a follow-up survey once the job is completed. Remember our goal is to annuitize our clients for future business.

Sometimes the never ending mailings will seem fruitless. However now that you have a computer, fax machine, and secretary that is geared to the things you want, these tasks will be accomplished with the greatest of ease.

As you are developing a relationship with the client, there are a few other ways of keeping your name in front of them. On one of your visits you may drop off some note pads with your company name and logo. It's inexpensive and allows you to have a reason for contacting them. Once you have them as a customer, free hats or tee shirts will put a smile on their face. Job site superintendents will always be pleased after receiving one of these. Besides that, it could help push your paper work through when billing time comes around.

After the job is completed, make sure a "thank you" note or card goes out at the very minimum. You must do this for the good clients as well as the ones that you didn't care for. For special clients, bouquets of flowers, gift baskets, gift certificates to a special restaurant, or theater tickets is always a nice gesture. As the holiday season draws near, don't forget the appropriate card. As I have said before, this continues to elevate their perception about you and your firm. The main reason for sending a "thank you" note is that you are thankful for their business.

Summary: Using letters via fax or mail for long term communication is of the utmost importance.

✔ ACTION PLAN

Assemble and write a master file of letters for almost any occasion.

THANK YOU FOR MEETING WITH ME LETTER

January 1, 1995

Mr. Ted Smith
Purchasing Agent
ACME Builders
54321 Shady Tree Lane
Any Town, CA 99999

Dear Ted,

Thank you for meeting with me today.

We recognize irrigation services as being a significant investment which, when properly performed, will return dividends for years to come.

Through stringent quality standards, ABC Irrigation maximizes your project's marketability and ensures enduring value from your landscape investment. We assume that responsibility with pride.

Thank you for placing us on your bid list. We will be pleased to bid on any projects in the greater metropolitan area.

I look forward to hearing from you.

Best regards,

Dave Jones
Account Executive

THANKS FOR OPPORTUNITY TO BID

January 1, 1995

Mr. Ted Smith
Purchasing Agent
ACME Builders
54321 Shady Tree Lane
Any Town, CA 99999

Dear Ted,

Just a note of thanks for giving us the opportunity to submit our proposal for the irrigation project called

_____.

I am confident that the services we render will exceed your expectations and am looking forward to working closely with your firm.

Please call me if there is any way that I can be of further service.

Warmly,

Dave Jones
Account Executive

FIRST APPOINTMENT CALL LETTER

January 1, 1995

Mr. Ted Smith
Purchasing Agent
ACME Builders
54321 Shady Tree Lane
Any Town, CA 99999

Dear Ted,

Our objective is not to do business with every commercial development company. We prefer to have few clients and many projects with each. We handpick our clients in much the same way that you pick vendors. We want to *service* them with the best of our abilities, exactly the way you want to be *serviced*. My firm is unable to do that with a broad client base.

We are a quality-oriented firm. We will not cut corners for cost savings or deviate from architectural specifications.

What else sets us apart from the rest? Trained personnel, who are sticklers for time schedules and committed to costs and response time.

In addition, we offer a single source of responsibility. You won't be faced with dealing with different players at each stage of the project. I will be the account executive assigned to service your needs and will be your only source of contact.

I will be calling you next week to set up an appointment for a personal interview.

Warmest regards,

Dave Jones
Account Executive

INTRODUCTION LETTER

January 1, 1995

Mr. Ted Smith
Purchasing Agent
ACME Builders
54321 Shady Tree Lane
Any Town, CA 99999

Dear Ted,

 Here is a list of project references and other pertinent information for your review. We are interested in being placed on your coveted bid list.

 We recognize irrigation services as being a significant investment which, when properly performed, will return dividends for years to come. Through stringent quality standards, ABC Irrigation maximizes your project's marketability and insures enduring value from your landscape investment. We assume that responsibility with pride.

 Should you have projects for us to bid immediately, please contact me at our corporate office at 555-5555, extension 101. I look forward to hearing from you.

Sincerely,

Dave Jones
Account Executive

Enc.

ASSURANCE LETTER

January 1, 1995

Mr. Ted Smith
Purchasing Agent
ACME Builders
54321 Shady Tree Lane
Any Town, CA 99999

Dear Ted,

    Since the bid date of the _____ project is fast approaching, please contact me at 123-4567 as soon as a set of prints with the changes becomes available.

    Due to the short time frame, I will be putting two extra estimators on your job to insure a quick turnaround.

    Should you have any questions, please call.

Sincerely,

Dave Jones
Account Executive

THANKS FOR HELP LETTER

January 1, 1995

Mr. Ted Smith
Purchasing Agent
ACME Builders
54321 Shady Tree Lane
Any Town, CA 99999

Dear Ted,

Thank you for the assistance on the _____ project. Your insight was extremely helpful.

Our firm's 25 years of working in the metropolitan area with developers and contractors has given us the ability to assemble a competitive and attractive bid. Your proposal will be submitted on or before_____.

I am looking forward to working with you on this project.

Warmest regards,

Dave Jones
Account Executive

INTRODUCTION TO LANDSCAPE ARCHITECT

January 1, 1995

John Smith
Appleby and Associates
12345 Oak Leaf Way
Any Where, CA 99999

Dear Mr. Smith,

Thank you for the time you allowed us to introduce our irrigation services to you.

The enclosed information provides you with a brief overview of our *25 years of-award winning* landscape services for both custom residential and commercial applications.

We are proud of our IA and State Association trade affiliations, and appreciate the opportunity to show you our performance and demonstrate the value we provide to landscape architects.

We would be pleased to show you our project sites and let you see firsthand the quality of our professionally-irrigated installations. An extensive project reference list accompanies this letter for your use to contact our clients.

We know it is critical to first understand what is important to you before we can do a good job for you. Let us prove to you how much difference a listening ear can make in the success of your landscape projects.

Sincerely,

Dave Jones
Account Executive

Enc.

COVER LETTER WITH PROPOSAL TO HOMEOWNER

January 1, 1995

Mr. and Mrs. Appleby
12345 Pinion
Any Town, CA 99999

Dear Mr. and Mrs. Appleby,

Thank you for the opportunity to submit our proposal for installing the irrigation for your new home in Ocean Crest. We are excited about working with you to create an efficient new system for your enjoyment.

This proposal is a result of the conversation we had at our meeting last week. I think you will find this new design encompasses everything that we discussed, and at a price that you can afford.

Please consider us as a valuable consultant working with you to produce a dependable sprinkler system you can be proud of for years to come.

I look forward to your questions and an opportunity to prove our high level of service to you.

Sincerely,

Dave Jones
Sales Representative

Step 19

JOB COMPLETION SURVEY

Whenever a job is completed, a post-completion survey must be done in order to evaluate your firm's performance

Whenever a job is completed, a post-completion survey must be done in order to evaluate your firm's performance. You know the ones I am talking about. Let's say, for example, that you buy a new car, go to dinner at some restaurant, or stay in some fancy hotel,—when the sale is complete they want your feedback.

The reasons for this may be varied, but for the most part, they do this for two reasons:

1. The business owner is truly interested in the level of service that the employees are performing. With an analysis of the feed back, the management can make adjustments in the way they service their clients. By doing this they can increase the efficiency and the profitability of the operation. This in turn will increase the likelihood of repeat customers or referral business, which is what this is all about.

   Fully 80% of all marketing dollars are expended on acquiring new customers. Very little money is used to keep the client, once they have been obtained. It seems as if contractors are more focused on getting these clients through the door fast and furious while not treating them kindly along the way. Ever felt this way? If we would treat our clients the way we like to be treated, we all would be dollars ahead.

2. The business owner is trying to get some type of rating from an outfit like J.D. Powers and Associates. If the rating is high, the company is going to use this in their marketing campaign to show the rest of the world why, for how long and for what year they did well.

135

The other night my wife and I went down to the local harbor for dinner. When we were finished, the waitress gave us one of their surveys, conveniently, I might add, without a pen. Hopefully it was an honest mistake. I did not want her to fill out her own survey after we left, just to make herself look good to the management. The problem with the questionnaire was that for the most part it was a little too vague. When you write yours, which I encourage to you do, try to be as specific as possible with the questions.

Robin's Law: Whenever you have an opportunity to raise the level of professionalism for your trade, do so.

Once your construction job has been completed, the survey can be mailed to the client and should include a self addressed stamped envelope for their quick (hopefully) response; personally presented to them when the final job walk-through has been successfully completed; or someone from your company should call to get some facts about your service. *Never* have the salesperson who handled the job call them. Usually a secretary, or someone who was not directly involved with the outcome, should make contact. The reason being is that you are looking for genuine "from the heart" responses. Generate a list of 5-6 questions that would truly take only a few minutes of their time. Hand written responses are the best since they can be assembled in a referral notebook and used for future clients as testimonials.

The more specific, the better you will be able to fine-tune your operation

The survey taker should be able to jot down their response below the appropriate question. Having questions that give a range, like on a scale of 1-5, are okay for some companies, but I prefer to be more specific. The more specific, the better you will be able to fine-tune your operation. These should be done within a week or two of job completion. This is one of those incredible tools that raises customer perception about your professionalism. Before you know it, word will get around.

Some samples are:

- How can our company be of better service?

- Was there anything you didn't like?

- Did the salesperson, job foreman, etc., perform the way you expected?

- Were they able to assist you through the hurdles of the day to day construction activities?

- What could they do to improve?

Summary: Job completion surveys play an integral role in perfecting your operation.

✔ ACTION PLAN

Develop your survey prior to completing your next job. Whether you hand deliver, mail or telephone for a response, make sure you do it.

Customer Care Follow-up Survey

Thank you for selecting our company to install your lawn sprinkler system.
We would appreciate your response to the following survey.

1. Why did you chose ABC Irrigation?_____
_____
_____

2. Please evaluate our performance for the following areas.

	Excellent	Good	Fair	Poor
A. Design Expertise	☐	☐	☐	☐
B. Installation Expertise	☐	☐	☐	☐
C. Completion of all work as promised	☐	☐	☐	☐
D. Crew behavior	☐	☐	☐	☐
E. Clean-up after job	☐	☐	☐	☐

3. Comments_____
_____

4. Problems that need to be corrected_____
_____

5. Who would you recommend that could use our services?
Name_____
Address_____
Phone_____

Thanks again for selecting ABC Irrigation. It was a pleasure being of service.

Sincerely,

Dave Jones
Account Executive

STEP 20

POST LOST JOB SURVEY

Whaaaaat?

The Post Lost Job Survey sounds sort of foolish. I mean, why would I care about a job that I did not get. Well, the importance is that you, as a smart entrepreneur, do care. The outcome of these questions may shed light on how your salesperson handled the call, possible products or services that the competition is offering, or possibly a pricing addition error.

> *Robin's Law: Trust your sales people, but verify their activities!*

Speaking from personal experience, I found these to be most enlightening, especially when it came to the performance of my sales staff. If you do hire sales people, and you will, this is a form of measurement that will allow you to check up on their performance in a professional manner. Depending on the situation, I found that some of the sales people had not been timely in their response for the bid date. Or they were habitually late for appointments which made the client nervous about our performance and being able to show up on a regular basis without excuses. Another response indicated that the reason the client went with someone else was how our weekly pay structure was set up. It turned out that this had been explained incorrectly to the customer. I keep telling myself, "No big deal, it was only a $4,000 job!" But $4,000 and another $4,000 and another $4,000 really adds up to a lot of lost sales. Needless to say, I took care of that problem in a hurry. The point is, if you don't check up, these problems can continue indefinitely and cost dearly.

Most clients were amazed that I was calling and doing some sort of follow up. Remember, the construction trade has a bad image. Again, this will raise peoples perception of your level of professionalism.

Summary: Finding out why you are not getting work will help you create or find a niche that could be very important to your overall marketing strategy.

✔ ACTION PLAN

Write your questionnaire then have your secretary start calling to find out how you are fairing. Be prepared because this could prove to be very enlightening.

POST LOST JOB SURVEY (SAMPLE)

Proposal To:_____ Job Name:_____

Dollar Amount _____ Persons Name:_____

Salesperson Name: _____

1.   How many irrigation proposals did you receive?

- What was the price range of bids low to high?

- Where did our proposal fit into the range?

- How much higher or lower was our proposal compared to the chosen contractor?

2. What can we do to help you with preparing proposals that are easier to understand or more clear to you?

3. Explain briefly the criteria you used to select the successful company.

- Who was the successful company?

- How many projects have they done for you before?

4. What would be your biggest reservation in working with us on our first contract together?

5. If all the proposals were identical in price, how would you select a contractor?

NOTES

STEP 21

ALTERNATE SOURCES OF INCOME

Once you have successfully reached this plateau, you are probably wondering, 'What's next?' At this point I would like for you to be completely satisfied with the level of service, professional approach, understanding of the sales process, and profits your company is generating. Before you proceed with this step, you should fully understand and have implemented the 19 previous steps. If there are some areas that require more attention, now is the time to go back and review those sections.

As a business entrepreneur, building a stable business with a predictable stream of income should be at the forefront of your mind. I know you have probably used the term, "This darn industry is either feast or famine!" Your long term goal should be to remove or minimize the famine times and make them all times of feasting. A way of doing this is to "annuitize" your clients.

At this point you should consider reselling your existing clients additional goods or services. It is a proven fact that humans are creatures of habit and will repurchase from those that they feel comfortable with or have a track record of doing business. Once you have captured them successfully as a satisfied client, they will be very easy to sell one of your other services.

This step should be addressed after you have determined that your operation is ready for new avenues of growth and income. You must have the proper staff and

> Building a stable business with a predictable stream of income should be at the forefront of your mind

management in place before branching out. The reason is that new ventures usually require additional amounts of time, money and energy. The pitfall is that without the proper controls, you could end up paying less attention to your core business—and that is what advanced you to this stage in the first place. A case in point is a dentist friend of mine that was doing extremely well. As his income started to rise, he started to dabble in the real estate industry. What once started out as a hobby, soon became another full time job. Before he knew it, his dental practice was taking a back seat to his home building venture. Then the interest rates started to rise and meanwhile he was losing a lot of money. He then wished he had his old dental practice back. To make a long story short, he ended up losing both businesses. That is not the position you should be putting yourself into.

One of the unique attractions of the construction industry is that there are numerous other related businesses and services. Offering other related services to your trade will allow you to develop other sources of income and creating the *FEASTING* I wrote about earlier. These other "companies" don't necessarily have to be employees under your care. Although, they could be. You could find dependable subcontractors to fill the bill.

This list contains some ideas of services or companies that you might be able to utilize in order to service your client base better or fill in during "off" times of the season. You probably have a few ideas of your own that fit your particular region of the country.

- Swimming pool service.

- If you do new construction, landscape grounds maintenance.

- If you do maintenance, new construction.

- Landscape lighting.

- Annual sprinkler turn-on/turn-off service contracts.

- Installing "smart" house conveniences.

- Masonry: brick, block, stone, tile, concrete.

- Fencing.

- Outdoor furniture sales.

- Tree trimming.

- Garden center.

- Lawn spraying.

- Pest control.

- Sand bagging.

- Snow blowing/plowing.

- Firewood sales.

- Christmas trees.

- Backflow prevention certification inspector.

- Irrigation system auditing.

- Replacing old controllers with hi-tech water saving models.

- Small tool sales and repair. E.g. chainsaw, lawnmowers, blowers, etc.

- BBQ accessories.

- Outdoor sound systems.

Summary: There numerous ways of expanding your current range of services to increase your current income and resell your existing clients.

✔ ACTION PLAN

Find a trade or service that you feel complements your existing business. Do ample amounts of research prior to making any moves. Once you have decided, get ready for action! Good Luck!

Now that you have completed this guide, it is time to go back and start over again. Your ultimate success will be achieved after you spend time focusing on each Step and then implement the ACTION PLAN. All things worthwhile require motivation, persistence, energy, and action. Here's to your success!